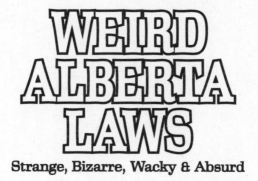

WEIRD ALBERTA LAWS

Strange, Bizarre, Wacky & Absurd

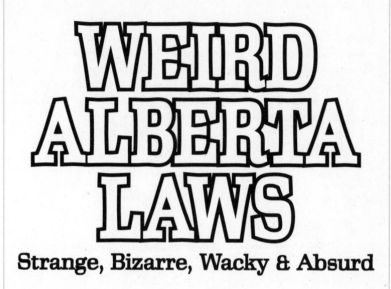

WEIRD ALBERTA LAWS

Strange, Bizarre, Wacky & Absurd

Lisa Wojna

BLUE BIKE BOOKS

The Publisher: Blue Bike Books
Website: www.bluebikebooks.com

Library and Archives Canada Cataloguing in Publication

Wojna, Lisa, 1962–
        Weird Alberta laws : strange, bizarre, wacky & absurd/ Lisa Wojna.

ISBN 978-1-926700-07-6

        1. Law—Alberta—Humor. 2. Law—Alberta—Popular works.
I. Title.

K184.7.C2W66 2011   349.712302'07   C2010-907630-3

Project Director: Nicholle Carrière
Project Editor: Kathy van Denderen
Cover Image: Roger Garcia
Illustrations: Roger Garcia, Peter Tyler, Patrick Hénaff, Roly Wood, Pat Bidwell

We acknowledge the support of the Alberta Foundation for the Arts for our publishing program.

We acknowledge the financial support of the Government of Canada through the Canada Book Fund (CBF) for our publishing activities.

Canadian   Patrimoine
Heritage   canadien

PC: 1

DEDICATION

To the men and women of yesterday whose missions it was to establish law and order in a new and untamed land. The statutes, ordinances and bylaws they penned provide us with a priceless understanding of our socioeconomic and political histories.

And to our lawmakers of today and tomorrow who will light our path to the future.

CONTENTS

FURRED, FEATHERED AND OTHER CREATURES

WORK—WHAT MAKES THE WORLD GO ROUND

Acknowledgements

When I penned *Weird Canadian Laws* in 2006, I was
astounded by the huge response I received from village, town
and municipal administrations in Canada. Shortly after
I requested information on any odd, unique or weird laws once
on the books, or still on the books, my email inbox and snail
mail overflowed with responses from communities across this
country. Without these individuals, many of whom spent time
after work culling through documents for me, I would have
never pulled together such a vast collection of information for
that book—it's simply impossible to travel to every community
to view their archives, no matter how tempting the idea might be.

As with the book *Weird Canadian Laws*, the feedback I received
to my calls for information on weird, different, strange or unusual
laws from Alberta was equally wonderful. Administrators, clerks,
mayors and councillors across this province replied to my email
query whenever possible. If the material I requested wasn't readily
available, these people went out of their way to try to dig it up
for me. Thank you to everyone who so graciously responded.

It has become increasingly popular for administrations to list
bylaws on their website, which makes perfect sense if you want
your residents to know and follow the laws of the community. And
so by virtue of the Internet, and the ongoing maintenance of
these municipal websites, access to current laws is just a finger-tap
away. All I can say is thank you to the administrators and website managers who maintain this bylaw information online.

In addition, I was blessed with an amazing find. Thanks to
Alberta Heritage and their digital project "Our Future, Our
Past," I was able to access a plethora of old laws dating back to
the time this province was still part of the Northwest Territories
between 1877 and 1905, when what was previously the District
of Alberta became a province. Individual municipalities participating in this Alberta Heritage project provided scans of original

documents, and perusing through these many thousands of pages has provided much of the fodder for this book. It took a team of individuals a great deal of time to initiate and kick-start this project, and they continue to collect, collate and maintain the information on this database. I'd like to extend a heartfelt thanks to everyone involved in this worthwhile endeavour.

At the same time, many individuals I contacted politely informed me that their community had no strange laws—in some cases, this was because a community had been recently incorporated and didn't have a lengthy history as an organized municipality. Yet, when I logged onto the bylaw links connected with their websites, I discovered particular nuances that piqued my interest and unveiled something unique about that community.

To clarify, the references contained in this book aren't meant to make fun of any administration, past or present, or their respective bylaws. They are, however, intended to give insight into the human condition—to provide a glimpse into how we think and interact and how we often need legal reminders about what, during our more level-headed moments, seems completely obvious.

I also feel compelled to thank you, my reader. I'm trusting that you understand my intention when I point out a law that makes perfect sense and yet question why we need something so obvious to be legislated. I trust you to laugh along with me when I highlight laws that addressed a need so out of today's reality it makes us laugh. I also trust that you might also question why a current law might be logical and necessary for one community yet seem completely unrealistic for another—coming from a prairie lake community where legislation surrounding the use of a common boat launch does not exist, I was quite intrigued to find other lakeshore communities had official legislation surrounding the use of similar amenities in their jurisdiction.

I would like to extend a generous thank you to my editor, Kathy van Denderen. Fine-tuning a project like this requires a sharp eye and an organized mind, and I can think of no better candidate for this job than her. A gracious thank you also goes out to Nicholle Carrière and the staff at Blue Bike Books for allowing me to pen another fun project and share a piece of Alberta history with readers. Thank you to my good friend and mentor, Faye—you are a true inspiration!

And finally, I'd like to thank my long-suffering family for their patience, yet again, as they tolerated my increasingly cranky disposition as the deadline for this project neared. Without you all, this and anything else I do would be meaningless.

Introduction

Scholars would agree that as long as human life has existed on this earth, some form of law or set of rules has been established to ensure we all enjoy a peaceful co-existence. Generally speaking, laws were always based on the principle of the Golden Rule long before it was known as such. "Do unto others as you would have them do unto you" seems pretty self-explanatory. Don't take something that's not yours—that means hands off your neighbour's car, Rolex, wife, child or anything else that might tantalize you from the other side of your white-picket fence. Don't hurt or kill your neighbour, no matter how irritating he can be or how desperately you'd love to wring his neck. And remember Sir Walter Scott's admonishment: "Oh what a tangled web we weave, When first we practise to deceive!" Trust me when I say that while it's usually not illegal, it's never a good idea to lie.

Of course, the person or people creating laws have a kind of supreme authority. That power provides its own double-edged sword, which is fine if it's God who is writing the laws. This omnipotent ruler of the universe is also all loving. So when He presented us with a set of rules in a nice, 10-point "bulletin," it was all in an effort to make our lives happier, healthier and less conflicted.

Of course, people being what they are, we routinely need every possibility spelled out when it comes to following the rules. Ten tiny little laws, no matter how all encompassing and perfect they might be, are not enough when it comes to the often pretentious, insubordinate and unruly human race. This was never more evident to me than when my son, who was about seven years old at the time, wrote a naughty word inside the silver memorial bell proudly displayed outside his rural, elementary school. Having committed his indiscretion in front of his three siblings, I was immediately informed of the wrongdoing the moment I picked them up from school that day. After an extensive pep talk with my son, I marched him into the principal's office and insisted he make a detailed confession of his crime. Once his punishment was delivered—he had to do some of the janitor's work while the janitor spray painted the bell—I thought everything was back on track.

A mother should never be too hopeful.

The nasty-word situation was still fresh in everyone's mind when a few days later I picked up my four youngsters from school and was told that my son had committed yet another indiscretion. He had decided it might be a good idea to write his name inside the newly painted school bell.

"Lord have mercy," I muttered to myself, wondering what it would take to get through to that child. As I grilled him about why he would do such a thing, I couldn't help but notice that instead of looking sheepish, as he did following his previous indiscretion, he was completely confused.

"Didn't you learn anything from the last time you wrote in the school bell?" I asked.

"But I didn't write a bad word," he said. "You didn't say I couldn't write my name in the school bell. You just said not to write bad words inside the school bell."

It was the first time—and I think the only time—I ever had to read one of my kids the riot act with such precise clarity.

"*Do not* spit, throw stones, name call, yell, start fires, break windows, hit people, scratch cars…" And the list went on and on.

"I didn't do any of those things," he said, ready to argue against any unfounded accusations.

"I know that," I said. "But I'm telling you *all* the things you must not do so you can't say you weren't warned!" I was trying to review every possibility, just in case he didn't consider how his behaviour might affect those around him. After all, a peaceful co-existence makes for a happy life, right?

Throughout the course of history there have been times when our desire for harmony and tranquilty clashed terribly with the art of reason, and the rules and regulations in any given community might have been taken a bit too far.

There might have been five minutes left of a movie, but there was allegedly a time in Montréal, Québec, when it was against the law to let the reel run later than 2:00 AM, climax or not. Closer to home, in Edmonton, it was once illegal for men to down a few beers at the corner pub with a lady friend. Certainly these kinds of legislation likely left many voters of the day wondering why they elected the individuals who presented such outlandish suggestions to their local council.

At the same time, it appears that most of us, like my son who apparently needed step-by-step instructions when it came to following the rules, need the details. If we want to live peacefully and travel the course of our lives with as little disruption as possible, we can't simply rely on common sense.

While we know buckling up children in a vehicle is the law, we still require details on when to graduate from infant car seats to boosters or exactly how tightly we should clasp our youngsters in. We need to be told that unless we count three full seconds at a stop sign, we've likely made a rolling stop and deserve that ticket we've just received. And although we don't want to hear the bass booming on the stereo next door during the wee hours of the morning, we sometimes need a reminder to keep our voices down when our neighbours are sleeping.

The collection of commandments, constitutions and witty writs in this book were culled from big cities and small villages, little known hamlets and regional municipalities across the province. Some are old laws that were pertinent when they were first passed but were eventually pulled or reworked and amended when they were no longer relevant.

Other, more recent laws might leave many of us scratching our heads, wondering why on earth something so logical had to be legislated at all. Still other entries represent odd laws that were quite likely unnecessary, even when they were created. And yet, surprisingly, the idea that spurred a law so captured the imagination of one town father or another to such an extent that he managed to convince his colleagues of its merit. If in the end we can get past the content of some of these bylaws, we might still stumble over how they were written—what exactly did the writer mean when he wrote that law?

Old or new, pertinent or obsolete, weird or logical, forward thinking or backward, in whatever category you choose to place any of these entries, one thing is certain: you're about to get a crash course on what not to do when living in or visiting this fair province called Alberta.

Transportation

*When man invented the bicycle he reached
the peak of his attainments. Here was a machine
of precision and balance for the convenience of
man. And (unlike subsequent inventions for
man's convenience) the more he used it, the
fitter his body became. Here, for once, was
a product of man's brain that was entirely
beneficial to those who used it, and of no harm
or irritation to others. Progress should have
stopped when man invented the bicycle.*

–North Wales author Elizabeth West, *Hovel in the Hills*

HORSES

When it comes to managing your mode of transportation, there's a lot to consider if there's a heartbeat behind that horsepower. Although you didn't have to worry about running out of gas when riding into town with your horse and buggy, you had to consider other factors. Horses can have a mind of their own. They can be spooked, rear up and turn tail, leaving a path of destruction behind them. They also leave a trail of deposits as souvenirs of their presence.

And then there was the rider to consider. Was his charge securely tied so it wouldn't wander off and trample through someone's garden? Was the horse protected from the heat of the afternoon sun while waiting for its master?

Fortunately for everyone involved, municipal councils understood the need to impose rules of the road for horse and rider alike.

Park It Proper

Folks riding their horses into the town of Innisfail in the early 1900s weren't allowed to tie them up on the north side of Main Street. The south side of the street was reserved for parking all horses and horse-powered vehicles, and while it might seem odd to us when viewing this law from a 21st-century perspective, it really was judicious at the time. It was all about providing a level of comfort for these creatures: the south side of the street offered the horses a modicum of shade, which was particularly crucial during hot summer days.

Put It Where?

Clause 8 of Bylaw 9, passed in 1911 in Hardisty, made it illegal for anyone to "place any carriage, cart, wagon, sled or other vehicle without horses upon any street of the said Municipality." The bylaw doesn't expand on this, but it left me wondering where people could park their horseless vehicles. Then again, it's unclear why someone would abandon their "vehicle," which must have made its way there via horsepower in the first place.

Designated Areas

In 1914, Ponoka enacted a bylaw that outlined exactly what the various pathways and roadways in town were to be used for, and how residents were expected to "park" their chosen mode of transportation in those locations. For example, tying one's horse to any "tree, shrub or sapling" would land you with a reprimand from the local constabulary.

The same was true for anyone riding a bike, horse, carriage or tricycle along city sidewalks: sidewalks were reserved for pedestrian traffic only. And if you were walking along that same sidewalk and at the same time pushing a wheelbarrow, you'd still be in contravention of this portion of Ponoka's public safety bylaw. No two ways about it—no wheels allowed on sidewalks.

Four-legged Mobility

Early settlers who owned horses didn't just keep them as pets they'd whistle over for the occasional foray through the country-side. Horses earned their room and board, and one of their jobs was to pull the family wagon into town from time to time. While the Mrs. and her youngins often held on for dear life as the wagon they rode in bounced along over every bump and pot-hole, the man of the household steered his unit into town to pick up supplies and do the weekly errands. Most gents knew how to handle their team, and warning other horse-and-wagon teams of their imminent approach in some way was a logical request for most.

Still, to avoid any misunderstanding and to implement a uniform method of announcing their presence, or to remind absent-minded or tired drivers, Lloydminster decided to address the issue head on. In 1916, the town fathers enacted legislation that made it law that all horses, mules or other animals pulling a sleigh or wagon had to be equipped with bells, and the drivers had to ring the bell loud and long whenever approaching another team or turning around a corner.

You can't help but wonder if the gentle jingle of sleigh bells was a tad benign when it came to expecting a quick response. Perhaps that's why the horn was invented?

Playing No Favourites

The first bylaw on the books for the village of Rockyford dealt with the "Licensing and Regulating the use of Drays" in that community. On January 5, 1920, council members declared it law that "every person having a Dray or other vehicle used for draying, hauling…" was required to purchase a licence to legally operate these "vehicles." Licences were valid from January 1 to December 31 of every year. If individuals obtained a licence after July 1, they were charged "two-thirds of the full charge for a year."

Harnessing the Horsepower

Once steeds pulled their charges into town, it was the responsibility of the person pulling the reins to secure the animals while conducting the business of the day. At first, horse owners tied their animals to whatever ring, post or hook was available, but that caused problems by sometimes blocking a path or sidewalk used by pedestrians. To rectify the situation, in 1923 the village of Standard adopted a bylaw disallowing anyone from tying a horse or horses to "any ring or hook or in any other way across the sidewalk, path or crossing." The original law did not, however, provide a helpful alternative for local residents, but it's a safe bet to say that appropriate hitching posts or local stables were eventually made available to help take the stress off the situation.

Knowing Your Place

It appears that residents in Airdrie may have had a tendency to ride their horses willy-nilly throughout town because the village council had to outline the appropriate places to travel. In 1967, Airdrie passed a bylaw limiting horse traffic to streets and alleys only. Horses were not allowed to travel on "sidewalks, boulevards and lawns."

Mind Your Mare

You'll no doubt want to enter this one under the "are you kidding me" section. It appears that horse-powered vehicle traffic is still addressed in the 2009 version of the City of Wetaskiwin's traffic bylaws. Under Part VI, the section entitled "Skateboards, Rollerblades, Cyclists and Horsedrawn Vehicles" states that anyone in charge of "any horsedrawn vehicle on a highway shall remain upon such vehicle while it is in motion, or shall walk beside the horse drawing such vehicle."

It may be shocking to some, but I can't imagine letting my mare and wagon wander about on the highway without holding on to the harness.

Pull Those Reins

In the early years of the 20th century, travellers making their way into the town of Peace River via horse and buggy had to keep their four-legged chauffeurs under control, especially when it came to crossing the Harmon River. In 1925, Peace River instituted a speed restriction of six miles (9.7 kilometres) per hour "while in the act of crossing over the Harmon River Bridge." This is barely a gentle jog for us bipeds, so the horses must have wondered if their handlers had fallen asleep at the harness when they pulled them back that far.

If anyone dared to push the issue, even just a mile or two, the authorities could slap a $100 fine on the negligent driver. If

you didn't have the $100 to pay the fine, you could find yourself facing as many as 60 days behind bars, "with or without hard labour." The Harmon River Bridge, which was also known as the Heart River Bridge, was located within town limits. However, the bylaw doesn't specify if the same speed restriction was in place throughout the entire community.

RULES OF THE ROAD

Canada might be a collection of provinces and territories that make up one happy family, but that doesn't mean individual governments always agree on what is and what is not acceptable. Like any family, differences of opinion are inevitable. This is particularly true when it comes to road travel. If you're planning a cross-country trek for your next family vacation, it might be a good idea to pay close attention to the road signs, and maybe even pick up the current driving handbook for the provinces you're planning to visit.

Closer to home, some of the current rules of the road in this province might, at the very least, make you wonder what chemical-induced, crazy antics led to their development. It might be the 21st century, but you'll likely agree some of our current laws are as strange as many of the earlier legislation created to ensure safe motorized travel.

Do Not Tow

This law makes a lot of sense, but it's hard to imagine why Albertans, or anyone for that matter, would actually need such a law—yes, I know, there are stupid people out there who make us wonder how they managed to get a driver's licence in the first place! According to the Government of Alberta Department of Transportation, you can't "use your vehicle to tow any person for example on skis, riding a toboggan, motorcycle or bicycle." Really? And why would someone want to be towed on skis behind a Beemer anyway?

Speed Demons?

It's a well-told joke, especially among our prairie neighbours, that Alberta drivers are heavy of foot. And there's a pretty good

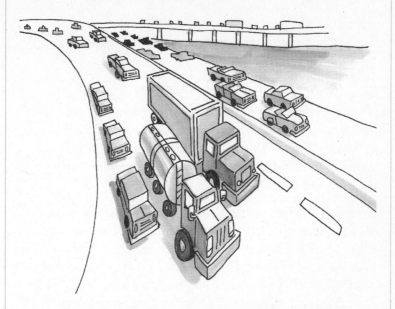

reason why we've earned that reputation. While many highways in the province post speed limits of 90 or 100 kilometres per hour, there are quite a few exceptions to the rule.

Although the driving instructors I asked were unable to explain why, you can coast along at 110 kilometres per hour on the Queen Elizabeth II, parts of the Yellowhead Highway and several other major routes scattered across the province. However, drivers have to rely on their keen powers of observation and a well-honed "take nothing for granted" mentality to avoid finding a ticket in their mailbox since this highway speed limit is not uniform throughout the province.

Some drivers coast along at 110 kilometres per hour on highways with a 100-kilometre-per-hour speed limit, and drivers travelling between Calgary and Edmonton push speeds of 120 kilometres per hour or more. Some habits are hard to break. So the next time you see a vehicle with an Alberta licence plate passing you in, say, Saskatchewan—where it appears most of the country's law-abiding drivers live if their propensity for driving *under* the speed limit is any indication—don't call them crazy speed demons. Just remind them that they're not in Alberta anymore!

Radar Detectors

Alberta is one of only three Canadian provinces (BC and Saskatchewan are the other two) that, at last count, hasn't outlawed the use of radar detectors in automobiles, which speaks more to our lawmakers' use of common sense rather than Albertans' perceived need for speed.

According to Martin Monaghan, a retired driving instructor with 35 years experience in the field, Alberta doesn't outlaw the device because there's no need to. "They aren't very accurate," he explained. "There are all kinds of radar detectors, and they say if you're going to purchase one, buy a more expensive model. But even with a very expensive radar detector, once it beeps, [the police] have already got them [nabbed the speeder]."

However, if you're still bent on buying one of these little gadgets, make sure you don't transport it anywhere outside the province. Police in the provinces and territories that have outlawed these devices can, and often do, confiscate them *after* they hand you an expensive ticket!

THAT OUGHTA BE A LAW

Driving slow in the passing lane.
Now *that* should be against the law!

Don't Hog the Road

Here's another entry for the "duh" file. It's illegal in Alberta for a vehicle to "straddle two lanes on a highway." Believe it or not, there is one exception to this rule, that being if the "conditions cause the use of a single lane to be impractical." Exactly what constitutes the use of a single lane as being "impractical" seems to be open to interpretation.

Buckle Up or Hold On

And the final entry for "I can't believe they have to write a law about that" can result in the wallets of both driver and passenger becoming a little lighter if this rule is ignored. The police in Alberta are pretty strict about seatbelt use, which means they also expect you to sit inside the vehicle. Not, as some might think is prudent, in the open box of a pickup truck or any other part of the vehicle's exterior.

Hmmm. Funny, but I never thought of sitting on the hood or trunk while my better half was cruising through town but, hey, I guess I'm getting old! Get caught in this kind of situation and both the driver and passenger could receive a fine.

THE AUTOMOBILE

The technical definition of an automobile is "a passenger vehicle designed for operation on ordinary roads and typically having four wheels and a gasoline or diesel internal-combustion engine." But for anyone who has ever owned a vehicle—which for our purposes will include trucks, motorcycles and mopeds—these wheeled wonders represent so much more than something that goes "vroom" along the local highways and byways. An automobile offers freedom: to work where one pleases, to visit distant friends and relatives, to take part in activities and to travel. Owning an automobile removes so many of the restrictions caused by time and distance, and in the past it indicated you had reached a certain level of success.

Perhaps that's why the automobile has always been so popular, even if only initially as a dream.

The quest to create this passport to possibility began as early as 1769, but it wasn't until the early 1900s that the mechanics required for ease of use had been more finely tuned.

Production increased in both Europe and North America, and seeing an automobile in your community soon became less of a novelty.

According to one source, there were 20,467,144 cars owned in Canada, or 74.1 cars per 100 drivers, in 2008. The number of registered trucks in this country, according to Statistics Canada's 2003 numbers, was 660,450. Add another 300,000-plus motorcycles and mopeds and there's no doubt about it, without stringent rules and regulations, we Canadians can have one heck of a traffic jam without taking into account our sometimes crazy weather conditions.

Mind Your Pedal

Before motorized vehicles overwhelmed provincial highways, the Alberta government enacted legislation regulating everything from appropriate licensing to speed limits. What made the May 9, 1906, legislation to "Regulate the Speed and Operation of Motor Vehicles on Highways" interesting were the extraneous concerns the authorities had to think about—considerations that would be the remote exception for today's drivers:

☞ The typical horn we associate with present-day cars and trucks wasn't initially a standard feature, and so our forefathers had to address the variances between different vehicles—motorized and otherwise. Spelling it out for Alberta's residents, the bylaw required every "motor vehicle" to be "equipped and supplied with a proper alarm bell, gong or horn, and the same shall be sounded whenever it shall be [reasonably] necessary to be sounded for the purpose of notifying pedestrians or others of the approach of such vehicle…"

☞ Vehicles also had to "carry in the front thereof a lighted lamp, or lamps, in a conspicuous position in such vehicle whenever in motion…after dusk and before dawn…"

☞ You couldn't drive your "motor vehicle" in any "public highway within any city, town or incorporated village at a greater rate of speed than 10 miles an hour, or upon any public highway outside of any city, town or incorporated village at a greater speed than twenty-miles an hour…" That translates to 16 kilometres per hour in town, and 32 kilometres per hour outside town limits. Of course, municipalities could adjust that speed limit in their jurisdictions.

☞ No one could "drive a motor vehicle upon any public street, highway, road, park, parkway or driveway in this Province in a race or on a bet or wager." It appears the need for speed isn't new.

☞ In 1906, pedestrians and other motorized vehicles weren't the only considerations licensed drivers needed to be mindful of. Horses were still the main mode of transportation for Albertans, and because a car trumps a horse every time, it was up to the "person having control or charge of a motor vehicle" to ensure they were always in control of "such motor vehicle in such manner as to exercise every reasonable precaution to prevent the frightening of any such horse or horses, and to insure the safety and protection of any person riding or driving the same…" These vehicles also had to keep a minimum distance of 100 yards (91 metres) between themselves and any horse-drawn vehicle.

☞ If you startled a horse coming in your direction and that horse caused any injury or damage to itself or anything else because it was spooked, this bylaw mandated that the owner of the motor vehicle was responsible unless they proved "every reasonable precaution was taken by the person in charge" of the vehicle.

Environmentally Conscious

It was against the law to leave your car engine running in Ponoka as early as 1914. Since the automobile was still a pretty rare commodity at that time, it's interesting that Ponoka's town council thought to impose such a restriction. Unfortunately, there are no details on the reasons why council members had concerns about the issue.

Keeping It Clean

Ponoka's town council also passed a law in 1914 forbidding anyone from throwing or placing "upon any of the streets, roads or lane of the Town any nails, tacks, glass, or hard substance having sharp points or angles, likely to cause injury to horses, animals, motor or bicycle tires, if passing over the same."

Watch the Speed Limit

The folks in charge in Lloydminster were on the ball fairly early on when motorized vehicles started making their appearance on local streets. By 1919, the town had already enacted a speed limit bylaw restricting vehicle travel to no more than 12 miles (19 kilometres) per hour. Although it's not altogether clear how the authorities clocked speed limits back then, they must have had their ways because a $50 fine was levied against anyone with a heavy foot. If a driver was clocked pushing the speed limit a second or subsequent time, the fine doubled. And if you couldn't pay the fine, you'd receive an all-expenses paid "vacation" courtesy the town council. The problem was, that forced vacation took place behind bars, and it lasted 30 days! If you didn't have the money to pay the fine, 30 days without work probably guaranteed you wouldn't have any cash once you were released.

Lock It Up

When cars first started appearing on town streets across the province, the idea of locking the car doors and pulling your keys out of the ignition likely didn't cross most drivers' minds. After all, what security did people have when they hitched their horse and left their gear in an open wagon while in town going about their personal business? That someone might hop on the saddle or drive a neighbour's wagon out of town was unheard of: why should cars be any different?

But they were. Keys in the ignition were just an open invitation for the more unsavoury sort of person to jump into the driver's seat and claim the vehicle as their own. To put an end to this kind of highway robbery, in 1948 the town of Cochrane implemented a bylaw making it illegal for car owners to leave their vehicles "unattended and unlocked." If you forgot to lock up or take your keys, and the authorities caught you, you could find yourself paying a $10 fine or spending 21 days in jail. Of course, this was only a minor part of the inconvenience if your car was stolen!

My Keys, Please

In 1955, the powers that be in Falher passed a bylaw "permitting the town constable to remove the keys from cars parked within town limits during the evening and night." It appears folks in that community hadn't heard about the 1948 bylaw passed by their neighbours down south, and by 1955 car thefts must have been on the rise. Drivers returning to their vehicles and seeing their keys missing must have experienced momentary panic. But once they realized the missing keys likely meant they were at the local constabulary, and not in a thief's pocket as their vehicle would have been missing too, they probably breathed a sigh of relief. That doesn't mean it was all clear sailing, however. The negligent vehicle owner had to "apply" to have his keys returned. This practice was considered a free public "service" to Falher citizens.

Get a Room!

If you're an RVer or if you've travelled throughout this wide country of ours during summer, chances are you've noticed the odd motorhome or two parked in a mall or grocery store parking lot overnight. It's a fairly common occurrence likely necessitated by the driver's fatigue and no vacancies in any of the local inns. Well, in 2002, the town of Jasper decided to put an end to what council members might have simply viewed as tightwads looking at ways to trim their travel expenses. The town council passed a bylaw that made these overnight pit stops illegal, regardless how many "No Vacancy" signs were flashing in town or how far the driver had to travel to the next available campsite. Park in that town hoping to catch a few zzzs and you'll pay more than a typical campsite fee.

Down to the Smallest Detail

In December 2000, Drayton Valley passed the third and final reading of its updated traffic bylaws. The newly compiled 48-page document covers every imaginable eventuality when it comes to traffic and the town's highways and byways. In fact, the "Drayton Valley Traffic Bylaw" No. 2000-09 is so detailed that it reads like the proverbial riot act, pointing out even the most obvious detail. Here are some examples:

☛ Did you know it is against the law for a driver to stop or leave their vehicle on any "thoroughfare, street, road, trail, avenue, parkway, viaduct, lane, alley, square, bridge, causeway, trestle-way or other place, whether publicly or privately owned, any part of which the public is ordinarily entitled or permitted to use for the passage or parking of vehicles," that would in any way "block, obstruct, impede or hinder traffic"? Of course, if your car broke down, this bylaw wouldn't apply, but why would someone would just park a vehicle in the middle of the road? Strangely enough, the practice must be pretty common because the same bylaw appears in several other community traffic bylaws throughout the province.

☛ If you're hauling something behind your vehicle, you'd better ensure your load is secure. That includes making sure liquids being transported are in leak-proof containers. You wouldn't want a trail of anhydrous ammonia tracking on the road, especially if you're in the vehicle following behind!

☛ Slow-moving vehicles such as tractors or other farm implements can't travel down highways at night unless they're sandwiched between well-lit escort vehicles on "either side." When I read this, I imagined the escort vehicles flanking a large tractor, with the three vehicles taking up the entire highway as they moved along, instead of an escort vehicle "in front of and behind" the tractor. If you ask me, it's this kind of muddy communication that gets a lot of us into trouble.

☛ Attention all operators of large vehicles; this one is for you! Did you know it's against the law to try to drive a truck or any other large vehicle "through any structure or under any overhead fixture, with a maximum height which exceeds the minimum clearance on a traffic control device for a structure or overhead fixture"? Seriously?

☛ And finally, did you know that "no person, whether as the operator or passenger in a vehicle, or as a pedestrian, shall do any act that does or is likely to intimidate, frighten, harass or startle any other user of the highway"? Get out!

People Are Important, Too

Pedestrians aren't forgotten about in Drayton Valley's Traffic Bylaw. Provisions have been made for their safety and comfort as well. For example, it's illegal to "crowd, jostle or harass pedestrians in such a manner as to create or cause discomfort, disturbance or confusion." If you're wondering how in particular you could cause "discomfort, disturbance or confusion," the bylaw provides several details, including these two interesting tidbits:

- ☞ Don't throw stones, snowballs, ice, or "other projectiles dangerous to the public."

- ☞ Don't block public access to any property or building.

In other words, try to follow the Golden Rule of "doing unto others as you would have them do unto you…"

Defining Moments

At one point in the City of Leduc Traffic Bylaw, a motorized vehicle is defined as a machine "designated for cross-country travel on land, water, snow, ice, marsh or swamp land, or on any other natural terrain." In particular, these vehicles include four-wheel-drive or low-pressure tire vehicles; motorcycles and related two-wheel vehicles; amphibious machines; all-terrain vehicles; miniature motor vehicles; snow vehicles; minibikes; and "any other means of transportation which is propelled by any power other than muscular power or wind."

I don't know about you, but I wasn't too familiar with wind-powered vehicles aside from, perhaps, wind surfboards that coast across the lake in front of my parents' cabin. But there are others, it seems. Apparently one can purchase a machine called a "landsailer," which also goes by the name of "dirt boat" or "land yacht." This surfboard-like scooter, which is equipped with a sail and looks a little cumbersome to operate, is powered by wind. This means you could use this invention quite a lot since Alberta is second only to Manitoba when it comes to the country's windiest provinces. When you consider these little suckers can travel at speeds of 105 kilometres per hour, don't cost a penny in gas and don't pollute the air as they move along, I wouldn't be surprised to hear that the City of Leduc council was considering a revision to their current bylaw to include legislation surrounding landsailers should these interesting vehicles start making an appearance on local streets.

Materials of Choice

Over the past few years, the economy has been on a bit of a roller coaster ride, and residents across this "wealthy" province have had to tighten their belts significantly, along with all other Canadians. Still, I can't imagine swapping out my car tires for a pair of skids or tracks. Going with the premise that laws are created because a problem arose over one issue or another, it appears someone in and around Wetaskiwin must have been boogying along the highways on something other than rubber tires because city council addressed the issue in their traffic bylaw, which was updated with its third reading in May 2009. A section of that document addresses vehicles "using other than rubber tires." It states, "unless a permit to do so has been issued by the Public Works Superintendent, no person shall operate on a highway any vehicle or trailer having skids or tracks."

THAT OUGHTA BE A LAW

Driving 20 kilometers per hour *under* the speed limit should be against the law. Here's my thought: people might consider hanging up their car keys and donning a pair of running shoes instead. It is especially annoying when these slow movers are toddling along on a two-lane highway during rush hour traffic. While it is apparently against the law to drive under the speed limit, I've never heard of anyone being ticketed for it. And I can bet my bottom dollar these "Sunday drivers" who are too busy goose-necking around instead of paying attention to the traffic cause unnecessary road rage and, subsequently, accidents.

Thumbs Out

This law isn't odd so much as it's laughable, and if you've ever lived in or travelled around the highways near Wetaskiwin, you'll know what I mean. That city's updated bylaw clearly states that hitchhiking is against the law. Yet it's the preferred method of travel by a particular demographic of the population—namely, people who prefer, or have no other option of travel, to walk or hitchhike. That said, I've yet to see a marked vehicle pulling over an offending hitchhiker to issue a ticket. Then again, hitchhikers are usually thumbing it because they don't have a vehicle of their own or money to buy a bus ticket, so issuing a ticket is probably an exercise in futility.

Three Birds, One Stone

On April 7, 2003, Drumheller passed an all-inclusive bylaw that dealt with vehicular, pedestrian *and* animal traffic. Some of the details of this bylaw differ from other communities, so if you're visiting or moving to Drumheller, you might want to take note—especially if you plan to walk, drive or operate a "vehicle of animal husbandry" in town:

- Back alley speed limits in Drumheller are only 15 kilometres per hour.

- If you enjoy daily walks and go with two or more partners, make sure your group keeps moving along. If three or more persons "stand in a group or so near to each other on any highway or sidewalk as to obstruct or prevent other persons from using such highway or sidewalk," they could find themselves facing off with the local authorities.

- Don't "stand, sit or lie on any highway or sidewalk," as you might obstruct other "vehicular or pedestrian traffic." Of course, you could get yourself killed too, but the bylaw doesn't address that possibility.

☛ If you drive a truck that weighs more than 6000 kilograms, or if you're driving a bus, you can't park it on any portion of the highways running through town—unless, of course, there's a sign telling you it's OK to do so.

☛ Parking a school bus on a town highway is also a no-no. The only exception to this rule is if you park it right in front of your home or a police officer gave you permission to park there.

☛ You can't wash your vehicle on a town highway or near enough to a town highway that the "water, mud, slush, or ice" slops onto that highway or any nearby sidewalks.

☛ And whatever you do, don't drain your radiator on the highway.

BICYCLES—THOSE NEW-FANGLED TWO-WHEELERS

OK. So they weren't exactly a new invention by the time our province was starting to define itself. German inventer Baron von Drais created what was essentially the first prototype for the bicycle in 1817. He named it the "walking machine" and built the entire thing out of wood. It was a one-off, though, and far from what it has become today.

Fast forward 100 years or so, and the bicycle had not only evolved considerably from its humble beginnings, but it was also becoming a more popular way for folks to get around. Of course, along with that increase in popularity came the need to introduce rules of etiquette, and safety, for sharing the road with pedestrians, horses and, eventually, motorized vehicles.

Take It to the Streets

Lloydminster was still considered a village when it first enacted legislation on the code of conduct for bicycle riders. A law passed in 1916 forbid bicycle traffic on village sidewalks. No smooth sailing along the boardwalk for bicyclists. They had to pedal their wheels over pothole-ridden, gravel roads alongside horse-drawn carriages and, eventually, the Model C and Model T Fords once these exciting machines made their way west from the Canadian manufacturing plant in Ontario.

Padding Out the Town Coffers

You know what they say—nothing is certain in life but death and taxes. And really, what is forking out money for a licence if it isn't another form of taxation? The town fathers in Fort Saskatchewan saw a moneymaking opportunity when it presented itself. After all, if car owners needed a licence to operate their vehicles, it seemed like a good idea to insist that bicyclists needed one, too. And so in 1945, it became mandatory for bike owners to purchase a licence for their bicycles. Owners who couldn't produce a licence when a peace officer asked them for one were slapped with a fine.

Check It Twice

Old bylaws on issues surrounding the use of bicycles and appropriate rules of operation were anything but consistent from one community to another. For example, the town of Westlock looks like it may have been a little more lenient than Fort Saskatchewan when it came to bikes rolling down their sidewalks or boulevards.

According to a bylaw passed by Westlock's council in 1946, anyone operating a bicycle with a wheel base 18 inches (46 centimetres) or larger had to drive on the street. No mention was made of bicycles with wheels smaller than the aforementioned dimensions, but it's hard to imagine a full-grown man pedalling a mini-sized two-wheeler just so he could travel on the sidewalk.

A Befuddled Bylaw

You can ride your bike on some sidewalks in Wetaskiwin, but not others. In particular, you must avoid pedalling along any sidewalks "within the zone identified in Schedule 'E'" of the city's updated 2009 bylaw. This bylaw presumes the 11,000-plus folks who live in Wetaskiwin have printed off a copy of the schedule and pretty much carry it around with them when they're out biking because there are sections of 50th Street, 50th Avenue, 53rd Street, 49th Avenue, 52nd Street, 47th Avenue and 51st Avenue where you can pedal on the sidewalks but there are other areas where you can't. Can you say *confusing*?

Who Knew?

It makes perfect sense to hold on to both handlebars when operating a bicycle. But if we all operated with optimum levels of coherent thought, we wouldn't need lawmakers, now would we? And so it is that the Government of Alberta's Department of Transportation outlines several safe-use dos and don'ts for bicyclists in this province. Here are a few of the more interesting, if not incredibly obvious, bike-related laws:

☛ Police frown upon people who routinely operate their bicycles with just one hand—or by using their knees, as I've seen many a youngster or high-performance athlete do. So if you want to stay on the right side of the law while riding your bike in Alberta, keep both hands on the handlebars and both feet on the pedals.

☛ One at a time, please. It is against the law to take passengers on a bicycle built for one—handlebars do not double as a seat for your friend. The only exception to doubling-up is if you're operating a bicycle built for two.

☛ The whole idea about riding a bicycle is to get a little exercise and enjoy the fresh air—or so I thought. Apparently this isn't everyone's outlook. Somewhere along the line, our boys in blue must have had to attend to enough accidents resulting from bicyclists grasping on to the side of a moving vehicle, presumably to get from point A to point B a little quicker, that they pushed for legislation making that kind of behaviour illegal.

☛ Three cheers for Mrs. Fletcher, the fiction-writing sleuth from the television serial *Murder, She Wrote*. She knew what she was doing when she equipped her bicycle with a basket and a ringer. (And to think my friends used to make fun of me for replicating that sporty look!) Although Cabot Cove, Maine, is a long way from Alberta, we're on board with decking out our bikes with that kind of necessary accoutrement. In fact, if your bike doesn't have a horn or bell, you can be slapped with a $57 fine.

☛ If your bike brakes aren't in good working order, you can expect the same $57 dent to your wallet. Of course, chances are you'll be slathering on antibiotic cream to your skinned knee long before the police notice your flawed equipment—which is perhaps punishment enough.

☛ It's obvious that your bicycle would need some kind of light or reflector if you're planning on cruising at night, but there were a sufficient number of cyclists who pedalled along city streets without one to provoke officials to take action. Those whom we've elected to watch over us outlined the must-haves in this regard: white front light, red rear light, red rear reflector and a pair of side reflectors. The cost to you should you choose to ignore this bylaw is the same for bicyclists who refuse to wear the life-saving headgear that's supposed to be strapped to their heads—$115.

THAT OUGHTA BE A LAW

You might not be able to afford a car, but let's face it, driving a bike on winter roads is just asking for trouble. Between the ice, the slush and the slippery roads, it's amazing more bicyclists don't find themselves as road kill—or cause multicar pile-ups for the motorists trying to avoid them. Ask around and I'll bet the majority of drivers living in Alberta would agree: biking in the winter should be against the law in this province.

Roll on By

In October 1989, Berwyn joined many other communities in making it illegal to ride a bicycle on village sidewalks. The exception to the rule was for children under six years of age riding a tricycle. Two-wheelers had to stay on the road. In fact, if you parked a bicycle on a sidewalk for more than 10 minutes, you'd be in contravention of this bylaw. The only exception to this part of the fine print was if a bicycle was "placed on the sidewalk for commercial display purposes."

Bicyclists Are People, Too

It appears that sidewalks in Drayton Valley don't have the same restrictions as they do in some other communities. Bicyclists are allowed to ride on sidewalks or "recreational pathways," but they have to "yield the right-of-way to pedestrians." Bicyclists are also expected to "yield the right-of-way to any vehicle on a highway, which crosses a sidewalk or recreational pathway," which is a no-brainer if the avid biker wants to live to cycle another day.

Hand Bells Needed

Did you know that if you're "roller skating, in-line skating or skateboarding," you're no longer a pedestrian and must yield the right-of-way to anyone you pass who is travelling on foot? Drayton Valley's Traffic Bylaw also states you must carry a "bell or other warning device" so that the pedestrians ahead of you can easily hear your advance—though it's not at all clear where you'd hitch that alarm on your person.

DASHING THROUGH THE SNOW

Two-wheeled vehicles move aside—there's a new kid on the block! The first prototype for a motorized toboggan was patented in the 1920s. But it wasn't until 1958, when Joseph-Armand Bombardier designed his version of the snowmobile, that the idea of a vehicle that sailed over the snow really captured the imagination of an increasingly wider public. Of course, that meant more and more of them were making their way around the countryside and, eventually, onto city streets. As a result, snowmobiles became yet another public concern, and councils had to decide how to regulate their use.

Turn It off, Would Ya!

The appearance of snowmobiles in Airdrie led its town fathers to legislate the manner with which folks could bring their machines into town. In 1971, council passed a law restricting snowmobile use in that community to between 10:00 AM and 10:00 PM. They also limited the areas where Ski-Doos could enter and leave the village—they could use the "east and west lanes" only.

Safe Snow Sport

Under the "everybody should know that but obviously don't" category, the Government of Alberta's Transportation Department has outlined several laws for safe, and courteous, use of snow machines in this province:

☞ Guess what? If you take your snowmobile onto someone's field without first asking permission to be there, you are trespassing. And as of June 2004, property owners don't have to go to court to press charges if they are faced with unwanted snowmobilers running rampant on their property. Today, a peace officer can slam trespassers with a $250 fine for a first offence and a fine as high as $5000 for a "second or subsequent offence."

☞ If you travel on public property, you need insurance. Hmmm...

☞ If you plan on riding in "ditches alongside highways," you can only do so during daylight hours and "only with special permission granted from the provincial government for a special event, or special permission (bylaw) from the municipal government." I think this means there are a lot of snowmobilers who could potentially face fines.

☞ Every snowmobile *must* have a muffler. If your machine's muffler has been "cut off or disconnected," had its "baffle plate removed" or is equipped with a "device that increases the noise," you are breaking the law—snowmobiles are noisy enough without this kind of helpful manoeuvre.

THAT OUGHTA BE A LAW

It's a well-known fact that if you don't clear your sidewalk of snow in the winter, and you don't comply with formal requests from your community administration to do so, the powers that be might clear it for you—and send you the bill. It's the law. And since turnabout is fair play, I think it should be a law that when the city you live in doesn't plow the road, residents should be able to hire a snowplow to do the job and send the city the bill!

Special Permission

According to Killam's bylaws, the only "non-highway" vehicle permitted to operate within the corporate limits of the town is the snowmobile. However, in 2006, the town council drew up specific regulations having to do with snowmobile use:

☞ No joyriding is allowed. Snowmobiles can be used "within town limits only when proceeding to and from the operator's residence." I don't know about you, but isn't this statement a little ambiguous? Most snowmobilers leave their residence and return home at some point during the day, don't they? The bylaw doesn't specify what is "allowed" between those start and stop points or if the snowmobiler has to drive around in circles before returning home.

☞ While tootling around Killam, snowmobilers can't exceed a speed of 30 kilometres per hour on the highway or 20 kilometres per hour on a lane or alley.

☞ Snowmobilers are also expected to "obey all laws and regulations of the Town and the Province of Alberta." No kidding.

Changing Tides

The ebb and flow of a society is reflected in its laws. For snow-mobile enthusiasts, the rules can be quite different from one winter to another, even in the same community. The town of Blackfalds entertained a number of laws governing snowmobile use over the years, but in March 1982, council members made a final decision regarding their use within town limits. Simply put, snowmobiles were a no-go, no exceptions allowed. An earlier bylaw, and all amendments to that bylaw, was rescinded. In its place, council passed Bylaw 509, "removing the privilege of allowing the use of operating snow machines on specific Roads and Alleys within the Limits of the Town of Blackfalds." End of story—for now.

Unlace Those Skates

Driving on roads after a winter storm might feel like you're on a skating rink, but that doesn't mean you should trade your vehicle for a pair of ice skates when making your way through Drayton Valley. At some point, someone must have tried to do just that because the town's traffic bylaw states that "no person shall ice skate or toboggan upon any roadway or sidewalk" in that community. Did I hear you ask for "new blades, please"?

BOAT TRAVEL

Granted, Alberta is a land-locked province. The rivers that flow within our boundaries can't compete with rivers like the Fraser in neighbouring BC. We're considered a prairie province—grasslands are where we excel as far as our geographic makeup goes. And if you come from Manitoba, like I do, and are used to lakes so vast you can't see across them, or land so wild you're never sure if you'll bump into a bear or wolf on your next paddle across the lake, Alberta's pretty dry. Let's face it, most of the lakes in this province barely deserve the label "pond."

Still, there are communities in Alberta that border small bodies of water. And in order to maintain their green spaces responsibly and provide safe access to the public, the administration and councils of these communities have had to enact legislation surrounding the issue of boat travel.

Boat Launch Bylaw

In March 2009, the town of Chestermere passed a bylaw dealing with boats and other watercraft, with or without a motor, "launching at the Chestermere Lake boat launching facility and surrounding area." Not only did this address the issue of resident safety, but it also provided the community with another means with which to collect levy fees. After all, a lot of public money goes into the maintenance and monitoring of a natural green space. It seems logical that the people who use the area help cover those costs—especially non-residents who don't pay property taxes.

That said, the regulations surrounding the use of watercraft, and the personal responsibilities of the owners, might be considered by some as extensive:

☞ Property owners using boat launch facilities for any kind of watercraft must register that item at Chestermere's town office. There is no fee charged to property owners.

☞ Tenants wanting to use the facilities must also register their watercraft, but only after providing the town with "a letter of authorization" from the landlord, since that person is the taxpayer.

☞ Property owners are only allowed "2 Boats and 2 Personalized Watercraft registered at any one civic address."

☞ Owners must display their boat launch decal on the right front of every watercraft. Property owners or tenants using the lake and launch without a decal from the town will be charged a daily fee. No refunds are given once that decal is acquired.

☞ Watercraft must be registered annually: registration expires December 31 of each year.

☛ Non-residents wanting to use the boat launch must pay $40 for their boat and $30 for any motorized watercraft, such as a Sea-Doo. If you're into canoeing and kayaking, or any other non-motorized watercraft sport, it will cost you $10 for the privilege of using Lake Chestermere—hopefully you don't have to rent a canoe too.

☛ And finally, no vehicles are allowed to park "in the regulated boat trailer parking stalls at John Peake Park [where the town's launch pad is located]" if they don't have boat trailers attached to them. I'm thinking this means you can't meet your fishing partner at the site in your own vehicle and park there once you're out on the lake.

Establishing
a Form of Government

*The best argument against democracy is
a five-minute conversation with the average voter.*

–Sir Winston Churchill

ELECTIONS— THE VOICE OF THE PEOPLE

There are laws for every aspect of life, and the electoral process is no exception. But it's interesting just how many laws are involved in securing the public's right to vote, and the fallout from that vote.

Nothing Is Free

These days, we take the right to vote for granted, so much so that come election day, many of us aren't concerned if we don't make it to the polling station by closing time—if we worry about making it there at all. But it wasn't always this way. There was a time when residents looked to voting day as a chance to be heard and to exercise their right to choose who would inevitably govern them in the years to come. So when Fort Macleod enacted a bylaw on December 18, 1900, stating, "…no person shall be entitled to vote until all His Taxes are paid," it was cause for alarm. It appears that this threat must have been significant to that town's residents because the bylaw was updated for several years following this original act.

First to Vote

Statistics have shown that providing residents with a chance to cast their ballots in an advance poll greatly increases the percentage of voters. The first time that Canadians voted in an advance poll was in 1920, when the country passed the Dominion Elections Act. However, this opportunity was reserved for "commercial travellers, railway workers and sailors," partly because they were often away and could otherwise miss out on their electoral right to vote.

In Alberta, one source from Cochrane suggested that the community actually beat out its federal counterpart by instituting an advance poll in 1919. The bylaw surrounding this decision offered railway men a chance to cast their ballot on any one of the three days prior to election day. Apparently, the law was repealed several years later, possibly because of the federal initiatives associated with the idea.

Some Conditions Apply

While most politicians do everything in their power to encourage voter turnout, Peace River had at least one reservation to their way of thinking. In 1920, their town council passed a bylaw "providing for the qualification of voters held for the town of Peace River."

That bylaw made one very large and loud stipulation in their definition of a qualified voter, and it wasn't about reaching the age of majority. The bylaw stated that:

*...no person shall be entitled to vote at any
election held in the Town of Peace River for the
purpose of electing a Mayor or Councillors for
the said Town of Peace River, nor at any other
election held in the said Town of Peace River
for any of the purposes for which elections are
required to be held by the Town Act of Alberta,
nor at any other election which may be held
under the authority of the Council of the said
Town of Peace River, unless such person shall
have on or before the first day of December
preceding the date of any such election paid all
Taxes due by him to the said Town of Peace River.*

This kind of practice is unheard of in this day and age, but if you
resided in Peace River in 1920 and wanted to have a say in who
ran your community, you had to make sure your taxes were paid
in full.

The Cost of Elections

Elections have never been an inexpensive affair, and the costs
are astronomical even when governments are pinching pennies,
if you can call it that. Officials estimated the cost of the
39th federal election, held in 2006, was a staggering $270 million.
And a returning officer hired to work on that year's election day
earned $200.87.

Flash back in history to January 13, 1937, when Falher passed
a bylaw naming a Mr. Patrick J. Demere as the returning officer
for the year. Should an election take place within that 12-month
period, Mr. Demere would receive a "salary of Four Dollars,
($4.00) for nomination day, and Six Dollars, ($6.00) for the
Election if any." It's a far cry from the $200 paycheque earned
by today's officers, but it was pretty good coin back in the Dirty
Thirties—especially when you consider that a local police officer's wage was a mere $60 for an entire year of service.

Making the Path Straight

Life has a way of running away on us, and even with the best of intentions, there are times when we don't meet our responsibilities because of the many stresses we juggle on any given day. Take voting, for example. Civic-minded individuals are well aware of the importance of making their voice heard and casting that all-important vote come an election day. But sometimes we get waylaid, and a trip to the polling station is cut short by some emergency or some distraction.

Fort Saskatchewan's town council thought that they'd put an end to at least one distraction in 1969. That year, the town's civic leaders passed a bylaw outlawing the "sales of liquor within the municipality on voting or election day." Residents in that city couldn't claim they'd had a few too many and lost track of time—at least not during the 1969 elections!

THE MECHANICS OF MUNICIPAL POLITICS

We are all aware that the governing body we elect oversees every aspect of our daily lives, from the amount of property taxes we pay to the apportionment of our income tax spent on health care or education. In a way we take this for granted—that someone, somewhere, is looking out for our needs. But the actual mechanics behind that well-oiled political machine isn't something many of us know much about.

This section is dedicated to the men and women who established a system of governance in the "new frontier" we now call Alberta. From our present vantage point in history, some of the bylaws that follow might seem amusing in their simplicity. And it's astounding to think a single individual often did the work several individuals complete today. Establishing new government is a little like learning to read—we need to begin with the fundamentals. While the laws that follow aren't "weird" or "strange," many were the first of their kind in this province. As such, these motions, action items and bylaws provide us with a glimpse into Alberta's rudimentary beginnings.

Putting Down Roots

Establishing communities across this province wasn't always preceded by a mass influx of residents or bulging town limits. Communities like Cardston, which was settled in 1887, started with just a handful of settlers. And although it was established many years before the district of Alberta was enlarged and made into a province in 1905, the southern border community is still relatively small, with less than 4000 residents. Nonetheless, by 1901, the forward-thinking settlers who built this town had successfully formed their first government. In a detailed first bylaw, the council laid out specific guidelines that members were expected to follow during meetings. Many of these items are similar to what we expect of today's council chambers. However, a few appear to be unique to Cardston:

☞ "No member shall speak disrespectfully of the authority of the country or use offensive words against the Council or any member thereof, or speak outside the question in debate, or reflect on any vote of the council, except for the purpose of having such vote rescinded." I'm wondering if this means that if a council member wanted a vote rescinded, he was allowed to use foul language or speak disrespectfully?

☞ A question or motion could be read as many times as a council member deemed necessary, but he couldn't ask for it to be read when another member was speaking. Really?

☞ Members were only allowed to speak twice on the same question, and "…no member, without leave of the council, [was allowed to] speak to the same question or in reply, for longer than fifteen minutes."

☞ Proposed bylaws could not proceed through all three readings on the same night "unless by unanimous vote of the Council."

Double Duty

Fort Macleod council members attacked a number of their concerns in their seventh bylaw, passed on April 2, 1893. The bylaw outlined the "Duties of Tax Collection and Nuisance Inspection"—it appears a single individual was assigned both responsibilities. Wearing the mask of tax collector, the official was responsible for banging on doors to collect anything that might be in arrears. Here are a few examples:

☞ He had to make sure dogs had licences and had to inform their owners of their immediate responsibility to obtain a licence if their dog didn't have one.

- ☞ From there, the inspector/taxman moseyed on down to the local "Saloon-Livery-Dray" and ensured these businesses had paid their taxes.

- ☞ The official had to inspect all "Streets-Alleys-Lanes" to make sure they were being properly maintained and kept clean.

- ☞ He was to ensure no "rubbish or refuse of any kind" was on public streets and alleys.

- ☞ He was expected to check up on vacant lots and notify owners if anything was awry.

- ☞ And finally, he was "to take charge of the offices of the council."

Funnily enough, there is no mention if this busy fellow was being paid for his troubles.

Growing Pains

On May 6, 1893, Fort Macleod decided it had "become necessary to appoint a Clerk and Treasurer" for their council. That day they appointed Robb Evans to the task and offered him the comfortable salary of "one hundred dollars per annum." Prior to that time, it appeared that the council collected all the minutes and dealt with the paperwork required in running an administration on their own.

Safe and Healthy Living

Cardston's town council appointed their first health officer on January 6, 1902. Martin Woolf, acting mayor and secretary treasurer at the time, was assigned to that role until the end of that year. The very next day, council also appointed Woolf as the town's "Inspector and Policeman" for the year, for which he would be paid $420. He was also given the job of town assessor, a position that didn't come with a paycheque at the time. Still, it seems Woolf was a tad ADHD, or maybe Cardston's administration was a bit of a one-man show?

By 1907, Woolf was juggling even more responsibilities. At the council's January 3 meeting, members passed Bylaw 103, naming Woolf the "Secretary Treasurer, Policeman, Assessor, Licence Inspector and poundkeeper for the Town for Cardston." The compensation he received for the entire commitment was $1020 per year. The bylaw was signed by the mayor and, of course, the town's secretary treasurer, Martin Woolf. I'm thinking, these days, conducting town business in this way might be seen as a conflict of interest?

Healthy Living and Legalese

The town council in Cardston appointed H.W. Brant to the position of health officer in 1907 for an annual salary of $25. At that same meeting, W. Laurie was appointed the town's solicitor for that year. His annual salary was $150—the modern-day equivalent of spending one hour, if you're lucky, with a new lawyer who has just passed the bar.

Paying the Politicians

On December 17, 1907, councillors in Cardston enacted a bylaw stating that members of council and their mayor would be paid $1.50 "for each meeting actually attended by them during the year, providing that the number of meetings for which any of them be paid shall not exceed twelve." What's interesting about this bylaw is that in effect, it dealt with back pay since it was intended to apply to "paying the members of the municipal council for the year 1907."

In the Beginning

Airdrie was incorporated as a village on September 10, 1909. On November 2, 1909, the members of the village's first council gathered to take the first steps in getting organized. At that inaugural meeting, M. Vincent was appointed chairman. R.J. Hawkey was appointed secretary treasurer and was given approval to acquire "sufficient supplies for Village of Airdrie." H. Edridge was appointed the village poundkeeper and constable, and according to the minutes, it appears that he had his first job assignment at that meeting: council members passed their first "action" request, stating that "all owners of cattle after Dec. 1 shall not allow same to run at large." Clearly, Airdrie's founding fathers took their responsibility of bringing order to this new community seriously and were anxious to get started!

Where's the Water?

Airdrie approved the digging of its first well during their November 30, 1909, council meeting. A promissory note was provided to the well diggers "to be drawn at three months bearing interest at 8%." The actual cost of the well was not mentioned.

At that same meeting, the corral of a man named S. Bushfield was chosen to serve as the town pound. The dear man received $5 per month for his troubles.

Legal Wranglings

On May 12, 1911, Airdrie's council decided the time had come for their growing community to have its own Justice of the Peace. After muddling along without someone in that position, council made the historic decision to appoint their secretary to write the Attorney General with their request.

Somebody's Got to Do It

Crossfield passed a bylaw to "appoint and regulate a scavenger" for their town on May 21, 1913. Hugh McBean was the poor fellow who pulled the short straw and landed that position. His job description included removing "all garbage, swill, slops, decaying animal and vegetable matter and all other rubbish, also to empty and clean all dry earth and chemical closets, cesspools and privies." His compensation for these unenviable tasks was 50 cents per month for each "closet" in town, and 25 cents per 40-gallon barrel of swill or slops.

However, if good old McBean wanted to get paid for his efforts, he had to collect the money owed him from the "person or persons for which such services were rendered." These individuals reportedly had five days to make payment. Residents wanting to hire their own scavenger to clean out their closets were out of luck in this community. According to the same bylaw, "No person or persons other than such authorized and appointed scavenger for gain or hire shall remove or clean any soil, swill, slops or any rubbish" without first getting council's permission and paying $15 "to form part of the Village fund" for the privilege.

Order of Business

Crossfield's council had already passed several bylaws before they enacted a bylaw "to regulate the proceedings of the Council of the Village of Crossfield" on January 12, 1914. The six-page, 44-point piece of legislation outlined all the details of council. Here are a few of the more interesting segments:

☛ Meetings were held at 8:00 PM, but if there wasn't a quorum, it looks like someone might have been appointed to rally the troops as it were, since the bylaw made provisions to begin the meeting at the start of "any hour thereafter during the same day as soon as there is a quorum;"

☛ It appears that elected officials couldn't just resign. According to the bylaw, "Every member of the Council shall hold office until his successor is elected." There is no suggested procedure should a member of the council die while holding office.

☛ Crossfield's council couldn't host their meetings anywhere outside the village limits—no field trips for these folks.

☛ Meetings were expected to stay on track. No business outside of what was outlined in the agenda was to be transacted "unless all the members of the Council are present in which case by unanimous consent."

☛ "Every council member present at any meeting must vote when a vote was called."

First on the Books

Horses, cattle, hogs, sheep and mules, and the restraining thereof, were the topic of Airdrie's first official bylaw, passed on April 3, 1927. The owners of these animals, or any other animals found romping about "at large," would be charged for the offence. If they were found guilty, and it was most likely that they would be, they were charged a fine "not exceeding One Hundred Dollars ($100.00) with or without costs." It appears the

appointment of a poundkeeper and constable was insufficient to encourage animal owners to keep a handle on their livestock.

While that first bylaw made no mention of a jail sentence should the offender be unable to pay the fine, that doesn't mean there wasn't one. That same day, the village passed a second bylaw, providing "for the enforcement of the By Laws of the Village." Bylaw 2 explained that anyone found guilty of any of Airdrie's current or future bylaws was responsible for paying the fine imposed. In absence of any predetermined fine, the constable involved could invoke Bylaw 2 and fine the offender "a penalty not exceeding One Hundred Dollars ($100.00) and costs for each offence." If the offender couldn't pay the fine, a "justice or Justices of the Peace or Police Magistrate" could send his or her sorry butt to the "nearest common jail with or without hard labour for a period not exceeding 30 days unless the said penalty and costs or penalty or costs be sooner paid."

Signed and Sealed

According to one source, the first bylaw on the books when Falher was incorporated as a village in 1929 dealt with the adoption of a common seal. The metallic seal was to be bordered by the words "Village of Falher Province of Alberta." The seal was made official on August 5 of that year. While many communities today consider branding an important part of cementing their identity, it's a little strange that adopting a seal was Falher's very first bylaw on the records.

The Rising Costs of Daily Living

Speaking of bills, the village of Falher presented its estimated expenditures and receipts for 1937 during the council's regular meeting on March 1 of that year. The expenditures for the year were estimated as follows:

> Administration—$410
>
> Buildings—$25

Emergency—$158

Fire Protection—$75

Janitor—$60

Nuisance Ground—$25

Old Age Pensions—$72

Police—$60

Public Works—$350

Relief—$175

Sundries—$100

The grand total it cost the taxpayers of Falher to operate their village in 1937 was a whopping $1510—weren't those the good old days? The money required to pay for these services came from three sources: $1300 from municipal taxes, $85 from licences and $125 from "other sources." Just imagine if our municipal governments of today had such small concerns to deal with.

Cost of Living Increase

Things were beginning to look up as far as wages went for municipal staff in Falher. On February 28, 1947, council appointed a Mr. G. Bughaud as the village secretary for that year. His compensation was $50 per month—a significant increase from a decade earlier.

It's unclear what events perpetrated the change, but just a few months later, on June 20, 1947, Falher's council passed another bylaw appointing a new secretary treasurer. This time a woman was awarded the role. Sadly, Mrs. Therese Moulun did not receive the same rate of pay as her male predecessor. Her wage was $35 per month.

Wise Investments

In 1943, the hamlet of Conrich wasn't much different, at least as far as its population went, than it is today. But the council running its affairs appears to have been careful with its funds. On October 12 of that year, an open council assembled in Calgary passed a bylaw to invest $2500 worth of the hamlet's $3653.95 surplus in Victory Bonds.

Women's Work

In the earlier years of Alberta's history, women could quite comfortably be categorized as the quieter sex. Their voices weren't heard as loudly as their male counterparts, but they were there

nonetheless. It wasn't enough to say that behind every good man there's a good woman. Alberta's earliest female settlers conducted the same backbreaking, heart-wrenching labour as their husbands, fathers and brothers. Women also looked beyond their own needs and reached out to help others. One organization that outshone many others for its good works and forward thinking was the Alberta Women's Institute. Their good works were so revered that even when money was scarce, local councils were willing to pinch a few pennies to support their work. On October 8, 1962, Blackfalds was one of those councils. That day, council members voted unanimously to provide a grant of $15 for the Women's Institute UNICEF fund.

Elder Care

In 1959, council members in Blackfalds acknowledged a need to provide special housing for the elderly residents of their community and the surrounding municipalities. And on June 3 of that year, the village entered into a master agreement with the Municipal District of Lacombe, the Town of Lacombe and the villages of Alix, Bently, Clive, Eckville and Mirror in order to acquire an adequate parcel of land. The agreement was the initial step in the construction of the area's first seniors' residence and it developed an outline for its operation and management.

Major Purchases

Developing and maintaining infrastructure is never an easy or inexpensive task. For example, on September 10, 1962, Blackfalds passed Bylaw 251, authorizing the purchase of a new road grader. The second-hand—or maybe third- or fourth-hand—unit was bought from the County of Lacombe for $350. Meanwhile, the village's previous grader had been sold to a fellow by the name of Ed Zirk for the sum of $75. Not such a weird transaction, granted. But a little piece of Alberta law trivia I just had to include.

Taking Out the Trash

Back in the day, folks burned their trash, plain and simple. But as populations increased, and the neighbour's house got closer and closer, it wasn't safe to continue this practice. Besides that, burning trash smelled bad. And so it was that dumps were built and a system put in place to deal with waste products.

Of course, all of this cost money—quite a lot of money, actually—and it wasn't long before local governments had to impose a charge on garbage collection in their communities. On February 22, 1983, the town of Blackfalds passed its bylaw outlining the charges that community would impose on residents:

☛ Single family dwellings would pay $4.50 a month for garbage pickup.

☛ Multiple family dwellings paid the same amount for each unit.

☛ Mobile homes and fringe residential properties were also charged $4.50.

☛ Businesses paid $9 per month.

☛ Garbage collection charges had to be paid by the 15th of each month. A penalty of 10 percent was tacked on to any property running in arrears.

Purpose Statement

Banff defines itself as "first and foremost, a town within a National Park and World Heritage Site," and as such, its administration has developed specific guidelines about what can and cannot be built within the town and its surrounding areas.

In order for anyone to acquire a building permit, an applicant must first consider these guidelines in their proposals:

☛ New structures should be sensitive to their natural surroundings.

☛ "Rustic natural materials" must be used in their construction.

- ☛ The applicant must demonstrate an "emphasis on structural expression and strong roof forms."

- ☛ The proposal must indicate a "respect for the pedestrian environment."

- ☛ And finally, a new building must tastefully use "decorative details and finishing that provide relief and texture."

The design guidelines were created with the area's history in mind. Headlining these guidelines is an excerpt dated May 3, 1887, hearkening back to a House of Commons debate surrounding the establishment of the park: "These buildings will have to be subject to the approval of the government, to prevent any monstrosities being put there to destroy the general beauty of the park."

While these "guidelines" are not "mandatory," I'd wager that a builder has a better chance of getting approved if the proposal adheres to these design guidelines.

Margin of Error

Residents of Blackfalds need to be absolutely certain they have a problem with their water meter before approaching the town to have it tested. If a homeowner thinks his or her meter is inaccurate, and it is tested and "found to be accurate within 98.5% to 101.5% of the water passing through the same," the expense of the test or calibration will be the responsibility of the homeowner. This detail is contained in Bylaw 1084, passed on June 23, 2009.

Laying Down the Law

*Somebody recently figured out that we have
35 million laws to enforce the 10 commandments.*

–Attributed to both Bert Masterson and Earl Wilson

PUBLIC SAFETY

Public safety is most often defined as protecting the general population from "significant danger, injury, harm or damage" by either natural or human-made disasters or crimes. Early legislation in the development of this country included everything from outlawing spitting inside public buildings such as churches, if you can imagine needing to be told not to do this, to frowning upon public drunkenness.

Some towns, cities and communities in Alberta have bylaws specifically designated as a public safety bylaw. The City of Wetaskiwin further describes their public safety bylaw as a means with which to "regulate problematic social behaviours that may have a negative impact on the enjoyment of public spaces within the municipal boundary." Other cities address the issue of public safety under different designations, such as the City of Leduc's Community Standards Bylaw. Leduc's bylaw focuses on behaviour in public places, as well as the activities of people "on privately owned property and immediately adjacent areas" to public property. So if your home borders a park in that city, you'd be well advised to brush up on what's kosher and what's not.

Attacking Infection

In the first years of Alberta's formation, the monitoring of health matters was as much a public safety issue as it was a health care concern. Infectious disease spreads like wildfire when not contained—just consider the smallpox epidemic of 1780 and the effect it had on Canada's Aboriginal population. With this in mind, "An Ordinance Respecting Infectious Diseases" was passed on March 22, 1877. Included in the many details in this law was a reference to the best way to deal with living accommodations:

- Residents of homes where infectious diseases were discovered were removed—or at least the residents who were "fit to remove" were taken from their home.

- These individuals were placed in "tents or other good shelter in some salubrious situation." Their homes were then cleansed, purified and disinfected before they were allowed to return.

Prevention Over Panic

Fire prevention was a primary concern for our forefathers. Without the aid of fire trucks and pressurized water, dousing a threatening inferno was a momentous job, not to mention a dangerous one. And without the benefits of modern technology, fire spread quickly, claiming human and livestock victims in its path and destroying property. Therefore, communities would impose bylaws to deal with fire prevention.

Some of the finer points of these bylaws are obvious and logical, such as a section in Cardston's fire protection bylaw passed in 1902 that reads, "no person shall deposit any ashes in any wooden container unless it be lined with metal."

But Cardston's bylaw also addressed the finer points of fire prevention. In particular, the bylaw gave specific requirements for the placement of stoves. Installing a stove wasn't just a do-it-yourself project for any homeowner. There had to be a minimum of nine inches (23 centimetres) between "any stovepipe and any partition or floor through whitch [sic] it passes unless such stovepipe be surrounded in such partition by a ventilating thimble of metal or of brick, cement or concrete at least one and one half inches in thickness and of the full depth of such partition or floor unit every such stovepipe shall be inserted into a chimney of brick stone or concrete."

A minimum of 12 inches (30 centimetres) was required between "any stove in use, and any partition or wall nearest thereto."

The Roof Overhead

On January 6, 1902, Cardston's town officials also placed
restrictions on what was required on the roof over their residents'
heads. Namely, it was law for the "Proprietor or occupant of
any house more than one story high with a roof having a pitch
greater than one foot in three shall keep a ladder on such roof
near the chimney thereof." The bylaw didn't specify what the
ladder would be used for, nor did it require a ladder to be kept
on the ground in order to get oneself up onto the roof for
whatever emergency might arise.

Preventing Fires

I've heard of people, especially farmers, keeping a barrel of
gasoline on hand for private and work use, but note the quanti-
ties of explosives being addressed in this next bylaw. In 1914, the
village of Crossfield passed a bylaw regulating the storage of "gun
powder and other combustible materials" within village limits.
Residents couldn't be in possession of more than 50 pounds
(22.5 kilograms) of "gun-powder, dynamite, nitro glycerine or
other explosives," or more than two barrels of "rock oil, coal,
oil, water oil…crude oil, burning fluid, naptha, gasoline, benzine,
methylated spirits or other similar combustible or dangerous
materials at any one time."

Surprisingly, it appears that it was OK to keep these explosives
in a house, shop or other building, as long as you didn't store it
"under the stairway to any building or…in any such manner
as to obstruct or render egress dangerous or hazardous in case
of fire." Now I might be talking out of line here, but I'd say
50 pounds of nitro glycerine located anywhere inside a burning
building might render escape impossible!

Equally shocking is that in Crossfield's great desire to limit any
fire hazards, this bylaw prohibited anyone from placing or
permitting to be "placed within the limits of the said Village
of Crossfield any hay, stray or other like combustible material

uncovered in his or their crate, yard or lot of ground within six hundred feet of any building, and no person shall have or keep such straw, cotton, hemp or wooden shavings or rubbish in stack within the village without securely covering the same so as to protect them from flying sparks or other source of danger from fire."

Safety First

As they say, there's a time and a place for everything. And breaking, breeding or training your horse in the middle of Ponoka's business district wasn't something the town's council members looked upon too kindly. Strangely enough, these situations must have occurred with relative frequency because, in 1914, the town enacted a bylaw forbidding these actions.

Other communities in the province enacted similar bylaws, although at different times in their history. For example, it wasn't until 1939 that Berwyn recognized the need to outlaw people from breaking or training their "horse, mare or gelding," as well as exhibiting their stud horses in "any public place or in any of the streets or highways within the limits of the said Village of Berwyn."

You might be asking yourself what's wrong with showing off your stallion in a public place. I would have wondered the same thing had I not worked for a community newspaper years back and been approached by a local horse lover who wanted to put a photograph of his stallion in the paper's next edition. The photo was to accompany a 4-H article, but the owner had the ulterior motive of cleverly advertising his stallion's services. The editor quickly put the kybosh on the idea, pointing out that the graphic content of the portrait—now, how can I gingerly state this…the stud's "ready stance"—might be considered offensive by some readers. It seems my editor and these early lawmakers shared a similar train of thought. And to think I hadn't noticed a thing!

Douse that Fire

Walking into a barn with a "lamp or candle not enclosed within a lantern, or with a lighted pipe, cigar or cigarette" could cost you a significant fine if the authorities in Ponoka learned about your indiscretion. In 1914, that town's council passed a bylaw prohibiting such an action in an effort to reduce the possibility of a fire spreading through town. Furthermore, you couldn't set a fire within "fifty feet of any building." Blacksmiths were exempt from this law, as long as the fire was built specifically for the purpose of their trade. If you were building a house, however, you needed to pay extra attention to the fire portion of this new bylaw. The old way of filling the gaps between your logs, or insulating your roof with manure, was now outlawed. And one couldn't keep more than three barrels of gasoline or kerosene, or "25 barrels if stored in approved iron tanks, unless it be stored at least sixty feet from any building."

Additional fire prevention measures included building codes that listed the specific distance required between stove pipes and floor partitions, the use of brick and cement and the specifications surrounding chimneys. These details were so intricate that the council instituted a "Constable or Police Officer, or such other person appointed by the Council" to make at least an annual visit to inspect "all stoves, chimneys, and stove pipes in the Town." These "laws" weren't repealed until 1998.

No Cutting Corners

Barbed wire may have been the only material on hand, but if you were planning on building a fence in Ponoka in 1914, and your fence bordered a public walkway, highway, street or lane within the town's limits, it simply wouldn't do. That year, the town council passed several public safety bylaws addressing a number of potentially "dangerous" situations, and barbed wire poking out as pedestrians ambled by the fence was deemed dangerous. And if you were diligent and used wood to build your fence, council members expected you to ensure no errant nails were protruding.

An Explosive Situation

In 1914, Ponoka's town council also saw fit to limit the amount of "gunpowder or other explosives" residents could have on their property, as well as how those explosives could be stored. This ammunition had to be stored at least 100 feet (30.5 metres) from any building.

Keeping Streets Clean

Perhaps the practice of sweeping your dirt outside seemed logical when nothing more than dirt was in front of your stoop or when planks were used for sidewalks. But at some point, the idea of shoving your debris outside with the swoosh of a broom became distasteful, so much so that the town of Ponoka addressed the habit in its 1914 public safety bylaw. In particular, business owners were prohibited from sweeping the dirt from their floors outside. Around this time, the "no sweeping your dirt on public sidewalks" became fairly common in communities around North America, which may have increased the popularity of the newly invented dustpan.

Fighting the Flu

Residents in Peace River were hit hard by the Spanish influenza epidemic. The cost in human lives around the world was unprecedented, and the cost of caring for the ill hit the northern community hard enough that they had to address the issue by borrowing money. Council passed Bylaw 42 on June 16, 1919. The bylaw made provisions for the village to borrow $4200 to help cover the $5244.44 debt incurred in fighting the deadly flu. Under the limitations posed by Chapter 13 of the Statutes of Alberta, the village was only authorized to "borrow up to eighty per centum of such indebtedness for the purpose of paying such indebtedness." It's not clear where the money to cover the rest of the debt came from.

Idle Hands, the Devil's Workshop?

Standing around and doing nothing could land you with a fine, or worse, in the village of Standard. In 1923, the town's council passed a bylaw prohibiting groups of people from loitering. The old law didn't go into great details about what constituted loitering, but you might suspect hosting a protest rally would have produced some kind of reprimand from the authorities.

Prohibiting Projectiles

If you were found discharging a weapon of any kind, including firearms, rifles, sling shots or "other implements [used] to hurl missiles," in the town of Bruderheim in 1941, you'd be fined $25. The bylaw came into effect on October 23 of that year.

Putting Out Fires

Grande Prairie might consider itself a rural northern city, but it's still a city nonetheless. Digging a pit in your backyard and stoking a small fire so your youngsters can roast marshmallows, an activity often done on an acreage, is strictly frowned upon within city limits. In 1989, city council passed a bylaw to "prohibit open burning within the corporate limits of the city of Grande Prairie." Now, that's not to say you can't have a wiener roast in your backyard. You just need to go about it in the appropriate manner. You must use the right equipment, which in this case means acquiring some kind of approved fire pit. If you are a tenant, you need to obtain permission from your landlord. And finally, you must purchase a fire permit from the city.

Fireworks Forbidden

The municipality of Jasper is strict about what business owners can and cannot sell in their stores. One bylaw states that it is illegal to "possess, store, use, sell or offer for sale any explosive," never mind to actually use them. Now, if local construction workers or road builders are planning to blast their way through a nearby mountainside, they have to apply directly to the town council for permission to do so. Once granted, the applicant has to provide the necessary munitions, which would mean either driving to purchase them or having them delivered, since there's no place to buy them in Jasper.

Quieting the Big Guns

Forget simple explosives, there are communities in this province that are outright waging war against the use of nuclear weapons and nuclear power. Fort Saskatchewan was one of the first communities in Alberta to lead the way in this concern by instituting a bylaw that would ensure a referendum on the issue was included in the town's 1983 municipal elections.

Details on the results of the referendum are sketchy, but support for banning anything nuclear in town must have been strong because council members forwarded a letter to their Member of Parliament expressing their "concern regarding nuclear arms and asking the MP to bring the federal government a referendum in the next federal election." Fort Saskatchewan council received acknowledgement of the letter, but details on its contents were not included in the minutes, nor was there any mention of receiving an official response or whether any follow-up actions were taken.

No Nukes Here

Red Deer took the issue of banning nukes a step further in its 1989 municipal elections. Voters were asked what they thought about council passing a bylaw that would make the city a nuclear weapons free zone. Of the 13,442 voters who cast a ballot at that election, 9571 agreed with the idea of creating the new bylaw and 2992 voted against it. Since the majority rules in these kinds of situations, city council put pen to paper to finalize the bylaw. According to one source, Red Deer is one of only five Canadian cities that have officially declared themselves a nuclear free zone. Go Red Deer! The other four cities are Vancouver, Victoria, Kitimat and Regina.

Don't Blow that Horn

Noise bylaws are quite common, though some have interesting sections that might give us pause to think a little. Such is the case with one bylaw out of the provincial capital. In 1925, Edmonton's city council passed an ordinance stating that residents couldn't cause any "unusual or unnecessary noise or noise likely to disturb persons in his neighbourhood." While this is completely logical, the bylaw continues to outline some strange situations. For example, residents could not "blow or sound or cause to be blown or sounded within the limits of the city of Edmonton, the steam whistle of any locomotive." Since it was perfectly legal for a train engineer to blow his whistle when travelling through the city, there must have been a few energetic youngsters with a lot of time on their hands and an inkling for mischief.

Squelch Those Flames

You can't burn a pile of leaves or your overgrown lawn within the corporate limits of the town of Hanna. Neither the neighbours nor the council take kindly to that kind of behaviour, according to the town's burning bylaw of 2002. Residents can, however, have "recreational fires" in their backyards, provided they follow a few concise instructions:

☞ There has to be a minimum distance of one metre between your burning pit and any neighbouring "buildings, property lines, or combustible material."

☞ The wood being used for fuel has to be clean, dry and unpainted—though it's unlikely anyone inspecting a fire would be able to tell if the wood had met any of those conditions before being set on fire.

☞ If a town official thinks the fire in your backyard is getting out of hand, and requests that you extinguish it, you must obey that request "immediately."

☛ And finally, the "fire, smoke or sparks must not create a nuisance or hazard to neighbours or neighbouring property." Now, I'm not quite sure how you would scoop those errant sparks from the air before they flutter into your neighbour's yard, but if your neighbour complains, you might find yourself up against the town's fire authority, and according to the bylaw, that "authority is the sole judge as to whether or not a recreational fire is creating a nuisance or hazard."

Sanitation Legislation

Wetaskiwin goes to great lengths to address the issue of sane and sensible sanitation measures in their public safety bylaws. In case you were wondering, these are not old and outdated sections but were included in the 2008 revisions:

☛ It is against the law for anyone to spit "at any person or on any public or private property that they do not own." In case there's any doubt about what is involved in "spitting," the bylaw defines it as ejecting "phlegm, saliva, chewing tobacco juice or any other substance from the mouth." Spitting in public will cost you $100 for a first offence, and $200 and $500 for a second and third offence within a 12-month period.

☛ One cannot urinate or defecate "in or on any public place or in public on any private property." The fine for ignoring this bylaw and relieving oneself in public will earn the delinquent a $300 fine for the first offence, $500 for a second offence within a year of that first offence and $1000 for a third and subsequent offence in that same time frame.

Aggressive Acts

Wetaskiwin's public safety bylaw also outlaws dangerous actions, such as tossing a large rock at someone walking by. The strange thing about this portion of the bylaw is that the fines for aggressive or dangerous behaviour are the same amounts as listed for urinating or defecating in public. And if the police catch you carrying a weapon or firearm, it will cost you $1000.

Feet Firmly Planted

Wetaskiwin's public safety bylaw goes into considerable depth when addressing the issue of loitering. Not only is it against the law to loiter in a public place but so is standing or putting your feet "on the top surface or any table, bench, planter, structure, or sculpture placed in any public place." The fine for breaking this law is $50, which doubles with the second offence and doubles again with the third offence that takes place in a 12-month period. Interestingly enough, the city of Medicine Hat uses the exact same wording in the loitering section of their bylaw to "regulate public behaviour."

Words Can Hurt

Being a good citizen in Wetaskiwin means more than avoiding
an armed conflict or a drunken brawl with your neighbour.
Taunting someone into a fight, swearing, destroying or defacing
property, shouting at someone strolling down the street or just
being an all-round dork could land you with a fine starting at $150.

Mind Your Tongue

The residents of Falher took a no-nonsense view of obscenities in
the 1950s. The town council passed a bylaw in 1957 "to promote
peace and good behaviour" in their community. That included
a ban on potty mouth. Swear in that town and it could cost you
$50 or land you in the town clink for as much as 30 days. What
exactly qualified as a swear word was undefined but, supposedly,
speaking without excessive care could cost you a lot of money.

The Full Force of the Law

Most Albertans are well aware of Vulcan's otherworldly reputation and attraction for Trekkies everywhere—especially during
its annual Vulcan Tinman Triathlon. But from what I can tell
after reading over thousands of bylaws passed in dozens of communities across this province, Vulcan made even bigger news as
having one of the most unique bylaws of modern times.

On February 28, 2005, Vulcan's administration passed their
bylaw "For the Purpose of Prohibiting the use and carrying
of cellular phones in different public facilities."

In this community, it is against the law to "use or carry a cellular
phone in the Restrooms, Washrooms, Changing Rooms or other
similar locations in Public Pools, Arenas, Parks and any other
public facilities." Now exactly how anyone would know about the
forbidden cell phone you forgot in your purse isn't quite clear,
unless, of course, you were snapping photos or talking while in
the stall. But if you are caught using your cell phone, the fine

isn't a few hundred dollars. No, no, no. "A person contravening a provision of this Bylaw and any other person liable or responsible for such contravention shall upon Summary Conviction before a Court of competent jurisdiction be liable to a fine not exceeding Twenty Five Hundred Dollars ($2500.00) exclusive of cost."

Fail to pay that fine and you could be locked up behind bars for up to 60 days "unless such fine and costs including the cost of committal are sooner paid." Highly logical, if you ask my opinion—and we all know how logical Vulcans are!

Mind Your Manners

Pincher Creek's administration takes the issue of bullying very seriously—and bullying isn't something that is just a problem with youth. Canada's Safety Council defines bullying as, "any incident in which a person is abused, threatened or assaulted… [and] would include all forms of harassment, bullying, intimidation, physical threats/assaults, robbery and other intrusive behaviours."

Bullying can come from family, friends, even strangers walking down the street, and Pincher Creek won't tolerate any of it. In 2005, the town passed legislation making it illegal to treat anyone unkindly or in such a way that the person, "reasonably in all the circumstances," would feel bullied. If you're found guilty of a first offence, the fine is "not less than $250." Second and subsequent offences could cost you as much as $1000 a pop. And if you don't cough up the cash, you could spend up to six months in jail.

Don't Touch That!

For some of us, our car is our chariot, our treasure and our baby. So for a stranger to touch our vehicle is tantamount to sacrilege. Wetaskiwin included protection of a person's vehicle in its public safety bylaw, addressing in particular the placing of "any leaflet, pamphlet, poster, handbill, flyer or any paper containing printed or written matter, whether advertising or not," under windshield wipers. This section of the bylaw also prohibits anyone from "depositing or throwing or causing to be deposited or thrown" anything else onto a vehicle. The fine for breaking this law is $50.

Naughty or Nice?

In an effort to "protect the safety, health and welfare of people engaged in, or receiving the services" of an escort agency, the city of Red Deer has outlined a fairly lengthy bylaw on the matter.

The Escort Service Bylaw details the process by which an individual wanting to establish this kind of business must proceed.

The application process includes information on the ages of workers, as well as other pertinent information, but the definition used to explain exactly what an "escort" or an "escort service or agency" is warrants a little more clarity. According to the bylaw, an escort is defined as a "person who for a fee provides a period of companionship for a limited period of time; provides private modelling, strip tease or exotic dancing; or provides any of the services offered by an Escort agency." Hmmm. Now to add a little more muck to the mire, an Escort Service or Agency "means any business which offers to provide the services of Escorts."

Straight Up Business

The city of Medicine Hat developed its escort services bylaw in 2003. Like Red Deer, an individual wanting to provide an escort service must first apply for a licence, supply all the necessary information, including a recent photograph, and pay the fee—and voila, business as usual. Operating the business without a licence will cost the offender anywhere between $500 and $1500.

House of Ill Repute

While Red Deer and other communities are a little more open to licensing "escort services," our forefathers weren't quite as liberal. Most communities frowned on the idea of visiting a "chicken house" or taking advantage of the services of a lady of the night. Edson's town council took the bull by the horns in 1912 and dealt with the issue of "common prostitutes or night walkers" with a bylaw outlawing the practice of solicitation for sex. Any prostitute found "in the fields, public streets or highways, lanes or places of public meeting or gathering of people" must "give satisfactory account of herself"—though it's not at all clear what giving a "satisfactory account" means.

Don't Be Idle

No, this bylaw isn't about loitering. But it is about doing nothing but blowing smoke. In 2008, the town of Jasper saw fit to institute legislation in an effort to keep their environment pristine and perfect, right down to the air that its residents breathe. Council members passed an "anti-idling" bylaw. Simply put, unless you're a postal worker rushing in and out of your vehicle to deliver mail or can provide some other workplace consideration as an excuse, it is against the law in this community to leave your vehicle idling. Break the law and it will cost you $100 in fines. Avoid paying the fine and you could be faced with any number of the penalties described in the Provincial Offences Procedure Act. In other words, jail.

Covering All the Bases

The term "litter" covers a wide range of offences in Pincher Creek. Under the town's Nuisance Bylaw, litter is defined as

"any solid or liquid material or product or combination of solid or liquid materials or liquid materials of products, including but not limited to: any rubbish, refuse, garbage, paper, package, container, bottle, can, manure, human or animal excrement or sewage of the whole or a part of an animal carcass, or the whole or part of any article, raw or processed material, motor vehicle or other machinery that is disposed of."

With that in mind, it's clear that dumping trash anywhere but in an appropriate receptacle or leaving your property in an unsightly state will likely land you with a fine. What is interesting, however, is that erecting any kind of poster on your own property can also be considered "unsightly" and fall in contravention of the Nuisance Bylaw. This is particularly true if the "placard, playbill, poster, writing or picture" is erected on property that happens to be adjacent to a public place or highway. You could also get into hot water if you neglected to acquire written permission from the town manager before putting up a poster. So much for the idea that "a man's home is his castle."

Strict Measures

Berwyn councillors passed a curfew bylaw in September 1942, making it illegal for "any children" unaccompanied by an adult to loiter about in public after 9:00 PM. The bylaw did not, however, explain at what point a youngster was no longer defined as a child.

Follow Your Daughter Home

Curfew bylaws were quite popular at one time in Alberta's history, and it seems like they're making somewhat of a comeback in some communities. For example, in 1998, the city of Red Deer instituted a curfew bylaw stating youngsters who even look younger than 16 years of age must be indoors between 1:00 AM and 6:00 AM. Further, a parent or guardian with legal responsibilities to that child is responsible for ensuring he or she is safe

at home. Parents and youngsters are equally liable here, and
should a peace officer escort your child home during curfew
hours, you can expect to receive a $50 fine—$100 if it's
a second or subsequent offence.

Talking Tough

If you think Red Deer is tough, check out Edson's take on
curfews. Youth under the age of 16 found wandering "in a public
place within the corporate limits of the Town of Edson" between
11:00 PM and 6:00 AM without adult supervision will find themselves in trouble with the law. This 2009 bylaw does make the
provision for a written warning for a first offence, and a $25 fine
for a second offence. Anything after that is $100 a shot.

Right and Proper Burial, Please

As early as 1911, the town of Hardisty got pretty serious about
the appropriate way to dispose of dead animals within its town
limits. Clause 2 of bylaw number four declared it was against the
law to "put any dead animal or the carcass or any part thereof,
upon any place within the limits of the Town of Hardisty so that
the same shall be in danger of becoming injurious or offensive
to the health of persons dwelling near…" and so on. Drop your
dead dog on the sidewalk and you received anywhere from
a $1 to $10 fine. I'm assuming this also means it's a no-no to
throw the dead animal into the nearest garbage bin.

Butt Out—At Least in Public

Speaking of dropping dead, or blowing smoke, the town officials
in Jasper are determined to keep their residents safe from second-
hand carcinogens. And so in March 2005, members of town
council passed a nine-page bylaw forbidding smoking in any
public building or any vehicle offering public transportation
regardless whether a "No Smoking" sign is posted or not. The
bylaw goes on to explain that outdoor patios are also off-limits

to smokers. This bylaw further outlaws the mere existence of an ashtray in public buildings and outdoor patios. Perhaps this caution is reflecting on the theory of "where there's smoke, there's fire," and council members believed the very presence of an ashtray might encourage someone to light up. On the other hand, the bylaw doesn't take into account the likelihood that desperate smokers in heavy withdrawal might just light up and butt out underfoot, thereby adding littering to their list of offences.

THAT OUGHTA BE A LAW

I always thought this should be a law, and now it is— at least in the city of Leduc. It is now illegal to light up a cigarette in your vehicle if there are any minors with you. Smoke with a minor in your vehicle and you're in big trouble! All I can say is, it's about time!

Locking Up the Big Guns

Dynamite, gunpowder and other types of ammunition were an explosive topic for Airdrie's village council back in 1929. The seventh bylaw passed by this community included the usual recommendations regarding the number of barrels containing items such as "crude oil, burning fluid, naphts [sic], gasoline, benzine, methylated spirits or other similar combustible or dangerous materials" that residents could have on their property, as well as the proximity of these items to homes or buildings within village limits.

Some aspects of this detailed bylaw, however, are quite unique. For example, residents weren't allowed to place the ashes cleared from their stoves "within three feet of any wooden partition in his shop, store, house, or any other building." It was also frowned upon to put those steamy ashes in the outhouse. It makes sense really. We all know what happens when you mix fire with natural gas!

KEEPING THE PEACE

Before anyone could inhabit a new community, countless chores had to be done. New buildings needed to be erected. Roads, sidewalks and other frameworks for a community to grow were just some of the infrastructure considerations a new system of government, once it was organized, had to manage. Doctors, dentists and teachers were also all nice to have. Then finally, once this and so much more was put in place, residents could relax a little. Kick back and let loose. And if there was a watering hole in the neighbourhood, why not enjoy a beverage or two?

Of course, it's also safe to bet that folks with time on their hands could get rowdy now and again, with or without the booze. If a community hadn't already hired itself a lawman, it was probably time to do so. Hopefully, it had also established a set of rules whereby residents could live together safely. It was time to take the "Wild" out of the Wild West.

The Devil's Temptation?

Gambling was outright outlawed back in the days when Alberta was still considered the "North-West Territories." No exceptions. According to an ordinance dated July 1, 1877, every "description of gaming, and all playing of faro, cards, dice, or any other games of chance, with betting or wagers for, or stakes of money or other things of value, and all betting and wagering on any such games of chance is strictly prohibited and forbidden." Well, now, that seems pretty clear!

Saying "I Do"

On August 2, 1878, the council of the North-West Territories acknowledged the right for ordained ministers and clergymen "of every church and religious denomination" to perform the sacrament of marriage. But the reading of that first ordinance

from today's perspective could provide advocates of same-sex unions with a little ammunition—although it's doubtful it would have produced the same result in 1878.

Section one of that ordinance stated that the authorized individuals "may solemnize marriage between any two persons not under a legal disqualification to contract such marriage." Those legal disqualifications were usually determined when the banns of marriage were read at three consecutive religious services and someone raised an issue about the future bride or groom. Exactly what those legal disqualifications were are not addressed in this ordinance.

Politically Correct?

There have been times in life when I might have used this next ordinance, passed on September 26, 1879, by the council of the North-West Territories. Entitled, "An Ordinance respecting Dangerous Lunatics," it declared that an individual who was "suspected and believed to be, insane and dangerous to be at large, and has exhibited a purpose of committing some criminal offence" could be hauled into court once apprehended. When the proof backing the claim was provided and the "alleged" status removed, the individual was deemed "insane" and was remanded to "prison or other safe custody" for an unspecified amount of time.

Checking the Privates

People breaking the law in Alberta in 1922 wouldn't just find themselves inconvenienced with a potentially lengthy jail sentence. When prisoners were incarcerated, they were thoroughly examined to ensure they didn't have a venereal disease. To ensure proper handling of this delicate issue, the province reviewed the various laws enacted on the subject over the years and completed the new Venereal Disease Statute that same year. If there was any hint of a potential infection, new inmates were examined by a physician within 24 hours of admission to determine if they were thusly infected. At this point in our province's history, venereal disease was defined as "syphilis, gonorrhea and cancroids."

The Stigma of Unwed Motherhood

A statute passed by the province of Alberta on April 12, 1923, addressed the issue of having children out of wedlock, as it were. According to the "Act to provide for the Protection of Children of Unmarried Parents," the District Registrar of the Department of Vital Statistics was to be notified at the birth of every child "born out of wedlock which is registered in his office under The Vital Statistics Act." At that point, the superintendent was

required to investigate every aspect of the child's life—children's aid societies were automatically contacted on that child's behalf.

If an unwed mother kept her child, if someone else gained custody of that child or if anyone assisted in any way in the "care and maintenance of such child" and had any concerns about the child, that individual was expected to contact the "superintendent for aid and advice in all matters pertaining to the child."

Of course, the generally agreed upon consensus seems to suggest that children who were "legitimated by the subsequent intermarriage of their parents" were in perfect and capable hands.

Tracking Down the Dad

Delinquent dads be warned! While an unwed mother was under the magnifying glass back in 1923, "sperm donors" who weren't stepping up to the plate weren't necessarily freed from their responsibilities. If an unwed mother named the father of her child or if the man was named by one of her friends or the guardian with whom the child was placed, the superintendent could "issue his summons requiring the putative father to appear at a time and place mentioned in the summons." It was then the man's responsibility to "show cause why an affiliation order should not be made against him."

It appears, however, that the quest to name a father wasn't a threat for the child's entire lifetime. The claim for parentage had to be made within the first 12 months of the child's life, or within 12 months of the alleged father making any kind of perceived acknowledgement to the claim.

For Whom the Bell Tolls

Nuisance bylaws across the country restricted noise levels affecting the general public, but in Peace River there was one noise that folks everywhere could count on hearing—whether they wanted to or not. According to Graham Smyth, bylaw enforcement officer with the town, Peace River's town council passed a policy in 1920 requiring the town constable to "toll the fire bell at 0800 (eight strokes), 1200 (12 strokes) and again at 2000 (eight strokes). The final eight strokes was the evening curfew bell when all minors under 16 years of age had to be off the streets. Following World War II, the town received a war surplus air raid siren, which replaced the bell. To this day the siren is sounded at noon, Monday to Friday."

Equal Recognition

Being barred from taking part in a particular function or securing a position of employment because of one's sex isn't something women today face—or at least not on a regular basis. But it really wasn't that long ago that women faced this type of discrimination. On March 31, 1930, the province of Alberta passed an "Act respecting the Removal of Sex Disqualification":

> *...A person shall not be disqualified by sex
> or marriage from the exercise of any public
> function, or from being appointed to or holding
> any civil or judicial office or post, or from
> entering or assuming or carrying on any civil
> profession or vocation, or for admission to any
> incorporated society.*

Although this became law that year and was made retroactive to
September 1, 1905, prejudicial decisions were still made in the
workplace until well into the second half of the 20th century.
For example, in the 1950s, my mother had to hide her pregnancy
from her employer for fear of being fired. While this act was
a step, women still had a long way to go.

Added Privileges

Women's rights were addressed to some degree in the
November 22, 1889, "Ordinance Respecting the Personal Property
of Married Women." At that time, the Legislative Assembly of
the Territories acknowledged that a "married woman shall, in
respect of her personal property have all the rights and be subject
to all the liabilities of a feme sole [an unmarried, divorced or
widowed woman]." But there must have been some restrictions
on the kind of property a woman could "own," as both the
territorial government, and eventually the government of Alberta,
revisited parts of these acts through the years:

☞ On March 28, 1922, the government of Alberta acknowledged the legal right for a married woman to be "capable
   of acquiring, holding and disposing of or otherwise dealing
   with all classes of real and personal property."

☞ On March 25, 1936, the "Act relating to the Capacity, Property
   and Liabilities of Married Women" stated a married woman
   was "capable of acquiring, holding and disposing of any
   property"; she could hold that property "in her own name";

she was capable of maintaining any "tort, contract, debt or obligation" arising from that property; could be sued without "her husband being joined as a party"; and was "subject to the law relating to bankruptcy." In other words, this liberating bit of legislature came with a price—no longer could a woman hide behind her husband should something go wrong.

Special Considerations

The Métis population of this province acquired new considerations when the government of Alberta passed its "Act respecting the Métis Population of the Province"—otherwise known as "The Métis Population Betterment Act"—on November 22, 1938.

The act provided the Métis of Alberta with an organization that would address their specific needs. In particular, the Métis were provided the same hunting and fishing rights as other First Nations people and were exempt from the restrictions imposed on non-Aboriginal peoples by The Game Act of 1932.

Harness Your Weapon

On June 24, 1997, the municipal council of Blackfalds passed a bylaw prohibiting and regulating the "use of firearms, fire balls, squibs, crackers or fireworks within town limits." From that moment on, it was illegal to discharge a gun or any other firearm within town limits. Now that's reassuring!

PLAYING NICE, AND THE POLICE WHO ENSURE YOU DO

Safety means more than the obvious. Following guidelines outlining the proper use of public property, for example, makes life safe for the community as a whole. For the police looking out for the public good, rules and regulations surrounding all aspects of society provide them with a roadmap guiding them in the best area with which to focus their energies. And when those rules and regulations dealt with something other than janitorial duties, which wasn't uncommon judging by some of the early laws passed in several Alberta communities, I'm sure law officials were overjoyed!

Taboo Pastime

Once upon a time, "nice" women didn't frequent pubs. It simply wasn't done. Perhaps this is why one alleged bylaw reportedly frowned on men meeting their lady friends at the neighbourhood watering hole. In fact, one source suggests it was outright illegal for "a man to drink with a woman in an Edmonton beer parlour." What's not at all clear, however, is who would be in trouble should a couple commit this dastardly deed?

A Heavy Workload

Peace River first established its police department in 1920. According to Bylaw 50, which was passed on February 2, police officers in that town were given the responsibility for a very broad interpretation of what we now view as "keeping the peace." When you peruse some of their responsibilities, you'll probably agree with me when I say it was a brave man who accepted this calling:

☛ The officer must take care and take charge of "all Town buildings and property and shall act as Janitor and caretaker of the Town Hall."

☛ He was also responsible for "...all the equipment, machinery, and other apparatus of the Fire Department of the Town, and shall be qualified to, and shall keep the same at all times in good order and repair, and maintain the same at all times in readiness for immediate use."

☛ In addition, he had to maintain the streetlights and sidewalks and act as the "Sanitary Officer of the Town," which meant he had to enforce all the health and sanitation bylaws of the town.

☛ It's not until the final instruction in the bylaw that a reference is made to the officer actually enforcing the town bylaws and carrying "out all other duties which by law are required of all Peace Officers."

☛ The poor, overworked officer was also expected to attend all council meetings and occasionally prepare and submit reports.

☛ He had to be ready to accept any additional duties council might deem necessary from time to time.

☛ Whenever there was more than one officer appointed by council, a Chief Officer of Police would be named. It would be his responsibility to ensure his underlings did their job— and did it well.

☛ And finally, if for any reason council felt the said officer wasn't satisfactorily upholding his responsibilities, he could be dismissed without notice.

24-Hour Watch

Incorporated as a village in 1904, Blackfalds had already been in existence for almost five decades when it passed a bylaw to "approve an agreement for the establishment of the County of Lacombe #14 Civil Defence Unit." Through this bylaw, Blackfalds' council agreed to work together with the county and town of Lacombe, as well as the surrounding villages of Alix, Bentley, Clive, Eckville and Mirror, to establish the proposed Civil Defence Unit. The purpose of such a unit would be to address "matters relating to civil defence and disaster."

Protecting Public Parks

Most people understand that town signs are posted for a reason. But Canmore went an additional mile to ensure that the rules and regulations surrounding the use of its parks was spelled out in the finest detail. For example, signs of operation don't just

LAYING DOWN THE LAW

apply to vehicle traffic in and out of a gated parking lot. Between
11:00 PM and 6:00 AM, it's against the law to physically enter
a park. If you're a night owl and want to walk your dog, you'll
have to keep to the city streets.

That same bylaw addresses the care with which the public is
expected to use public parks. And if you're the kind of person
who needs the obvious spelled out to you, it is against the law in
Canmore to "damage, deface, destroy, mark, burn, move, remove
or otherwise interfere with…a structure, fence, building, wall,
bench, exhibit, fixture, improvement, sign, or any other property
[along with vegetation, soil, sand, gravel, and wood] located in
the park." You're also not allowed to engage in any activity that
could injure or disturb another visitor. This includes shooting
golf balls, launching harmful projectiles or using foul language.
This lovely, detailed bylaw puts a whole new meaning into
being pristine.

Fact or Fiction?

This law is widely known because it has been advertised on
various Internet sites and is included in at least two collections
of weird laws. In fact, if you search enough Google pages, you'll
notice the "law" evolved at some point in its telling from just
being a strange law pertinent to Alberta justice to one that was
practiced on a national level. In effect, this law has become its
own urban legend. But is it true or false? I'll let you decide.

A handgun, bullets and a horse were supposedly the parting gifts
given to any newly released prisoner at one time in this province's
history. The reasoning behind this arrangement was to enable the
ex-convict a quick ride out of town and a way to protect himself
from any enemies he might have made at one point in his life or
another. Sounds reasonable to me, if not a tad overly generous!

THAT OUGHTA BE A LAW

We've all heard about road rage, but it appears another kind of moving rage is rearing its ugly head out there—walking rage! Yup. Waddle a little too slowly or take up too much room on the sidewalk or running path and you could be the victim of a steady stream of verbal abuse or maybe even a shove or two. Surely this kind of scathing behaviour is against the law—and if it isn't, it should be.

Steep Penalties

Eventually, communities figured out that if they didn't impose some kind of penalty on folks not paying their property taxes, those taxes would remain in arrears. As well, subsequent taxes would also most likely remain unpaid. So on January 21, 1952, Blackfalds charged a stiff, six-percent penalty to residents disregarding their tax bills. Furthermore, that penalty would be "added to all unpaid taxes and each succeeding year so long as the taxes remain unpaid."

Tough stand, to be sure. But the bylaw doesn't offer any insight on how long the town would look the other way, and just add interest to a bill, and at what point they'd finally step in and force the issue more assertively.

Private and Public Property

By Liberty I understand the Power which every man has over his own Actions, and his Right to enjoy the Fruits of his Labour, Art, and Industry, as far as by it he hurts not the Society, or any Members of it, by taking from any Member, or by hindering him from enjoying what he himself enjoys. The Fruits of a Man's honest Industry are the just Rewards of it, ascertained to him by natural and eternal Equity, as is his Title to use them in the Manner which he thinks fit: And thus, with the above Limitations, every Man is sole Lord and Arbiter of his own private Actions and Property.

–Cato, Roman statesman

PROPERTY LAWS

When homesteaders first traversed this vast country and started settling in Alberta, their immediate priority was to build some kind of shelter for themselves and their families. Exactly what that shelter would look like usually depended on the materials available at the time of year they arrived. Given that it was rapidly made clear that winters throughout the prairies were typically harsh and often unforgiving, new migration usually took place in spring and summer.

As more and more homes were built and communities were forming, it was necessary to develop building guidelines. A mud hut with a straw roof might have provided sufficient shelter for a small family, but it was also a bigger fire hazard than a solid stone or well-built wooden structure. Then there was proper sanitation to consider, such as developing appropriate ways of dealing with human waste—and all manner of considerations that, today, we take for granted.

Setting Up Boundaries

If you were against using poisons, another way to protect your property from the damage created by wildlife was to build a fence. As early as August 2, 1878, the North-West Territories enacted "An Ordinance respecting Fences" to provide residents with guidelines on what were acceptable building practices:

☛ A lawful fence was described as "four feet and six inches high, the lower rail not more than one foot from the ground, and no other rails more than eight inches apart, except the top rail of worm fences, and any river bank or other natural boundary reasonably sufficient to protect growing crops from domestic animals."

☛ When a property owner erected such a nice and lawful fence as described above, the neighbour whose property butted up against that fence had to automatically fork over half the cost. Both property owners were responsible for half the fence's upkeep as well, and if one or the other neighbour failed to uphold these responsibilities, that person "after one week's notice from his neighbour shall compensate such neighbour to the value of the work done in making and repairing the same."

Managing Materials

Building requirements were imposed on Cardston residents as early as 1902. By then, there was no tolerance for homebuilders using manure, hay or straw as roofing or building materials. The only exception to this rule was if the new home in question was being built a minimum of "one hundred feet [30.5 metres] distant from any other building in which a fire is ever kindled." Since it appears likely that during the cooler parts of the year someone was bound to light a fire, that criteria probably applied to every building. Furthermore, it was against this bylaw for anyone to stack grain, hay or straw on any property "within one hundred feet of any building in which a fire is ever kindled."

Laying Out the Land

I've never been to Cardston, but I'm thinking it must be a meticulously laid out community because that town's officials were planning their subdivisions as early as 1907, not long after the Province of Alberta amended their land titles act that same year. Bylaw 131 contains seven regulations on how land in the corporate limits of Cardston would be subdivided:

1. Streets couldn't be laid out "less than 66 feet [20 metres] in width."

2. Lanes must be at least 20 feet (six metres) wide.

3. Every lot had to have a rear access to the back lane.

4. The distance between parallel "streets or lanes" could "not exceed five hundred feet [152 metres]."

5. In the case of new subdivisions butting up against existing ones, members of council would work with new builders to modify the plans so that "a sufficient number of streets in either or both of the adjoining subdivisions shall be produced through the new survey, and the municipality council will determine what street in either or both of the provisions subdivisions shall be so produced."

6. If council determined the need to do so, they could vote to exempt any subdivision from any of the provisions of their regulations.

7. And of course, if anyone wasn't happy with council's decision, they had the right to appeal.

Swimming Restricted

Regardless of the temperature, or the desperate need for a bath, folks in Edson were not allowed to bathe or swim in watering holes within town limits between 9:00 PM and 6:00 AM. Take a chance and this 1912 bylaw would land you in hot water!

A Step Up

On May 28, 1912, Lacombe passed a bylaw that allowed the community to take out a debenture totalling $2454.51. The reason for this loan was to create a granolithic sidewalk along selected streets. In case you aren't aware, a granolithic sidewalk is almost like cement, composed of crushed granite and stone, for example. The extensive bylaw also outlined the repayment plan for constructing this sidewalk. Altogether, it would take the people of Lacombe 25 years to pay off the debt.

Dealing with Death

Death and taxes—the two guarantees in life. It's fitting, then, that a great deal of municipal business surrounds the issue of taxes. And although significantly fewer bylaws deal with death, they do exist. Take cemeteries, for example. The proper burial of deceased loved ones is often the first order of business in a new community. At least this certainly was the case for Crossfield in 1913.

The village's council passed its second bylaw that focused solely and quite extensively on the issue of securing land for a cemetery and the details surrounding the purchasing of a plot, the care and maintenance of the property and the conduct of visitors:

☛ Plots weren't cheap, even in 1913. It cost $4 for a single public lot, regardless if the plot was for an adult or child. Corner lots cost $10. Families looking to buy blocks of five or more lots were often offered first choice, though those considerations weren't spelled out in the bylaw.

☛ Once the lot was purchased, the owner was not allowed to make money on any interment that would eventually take place there.

☛ Families could erect monuments or cultivate plants around their family plots, but the plans had to be approved by council first.

☛ Even after the plans had been approved, if the council felt any "monument, enclosure or any inscription" was "improper or injurious to the appearance of the lots or graves," they could have it removed.

☛ And while some communities passed bylaws making it illegal to venture into a graveyard during certain periods of the night, Crossfield's policy was quite different. Family members were allowed access to their lots "at all times."

☛ A section of the cemetery was also established for the sole purpose of interring "the poor and all persons unable to pay the necessary expenses."

Ashes to Ashes

Wood-burning stoves were the primary heat source for families at the turn of the 20th century, so you wouldn't think disposing of the ashes would cause much of a problem. But the reverse must have been true because in 1913 Lloydminster established explicit guidelines on the proper disposal of ashes.

First, the homeowner had to acquire a metal container measuring a minimum of 27 inches (68 centimetres) in height and three inches (eight centimetres) in diameter. The ashes were to be shovelled into this container and remain there until cool. You weren't allowed to dump the ashes on "any street, lane, road or public property" in town. However, the bylaw didn't explain exactly what a homeowner was to do with the ashes after they had cooled. The fine for non-compliance was $10 or up to 20 days in jail.

THAT OUGHTA BE A LAW

Weeds. Let those darlin' dandelions dominate your yard and you could have the local bylaw officer knocking on your door and demanding you down their sunny heads. If you don't, the city, once again, can do it for you and charge you for the job. This might seem a little odd if you live in a community where most parks are a sea of yellow until well into the summer when they die out naturally anyway. Perhaps it should be a law that when local residents have to take care of the unsightly mess that will inevitably spread onto their property, they can charge the city for all their hard work!

Ditch the Straw

Concerned about protecting their community from the spread of fire, in 1914, Ponoka's town council passed a bylaw addressing the issue of building materials. Mud huts were to be a thing of the past, as were straw roofs and the use of "manure, hay, straw and other 'inflammable materials'" when building new homes. Somehow the use of wood as a building material wasn't considered an "inflammable" material.

Fee For Use

Residents of Cochrane could access drinking water from street taps as early as 1915, but a bylaw enacted that year put a price on the privilege. Residents were charged 75 cents for three months' worth of access. The bill had to be paid in advance of consumption, and anyone trying to circumvent the process and poach water when they thought no one was looking could face a $25 fine. By my calculations, that $25 fine could have provided the offender with at least 33 months of access.

Hold on to Your Hay

It was more than the town fathers in Lloydminster just wanting to keep their streets clean and free from debris that motivated them to create this 1919 bylaw. But the logistics of farmers trying to prevent "loose hay, straw or other feed" from blowing into the village must have been somewhat daunting, especially when you consider the kind of winds that frequently whip up in Alberta during summer.

It appears the loose bits of agricultural produce were deemed both a "fire hazard and a nuisance." Anyone unable to contain their straw would face a $20 fine and as many as 30 days in jail. What's not at all clear is how anyone could identify one bit of straw as belonging to one farmer or another, especially when the weather was extremely wicked.

Cleanliness Spells Safety

Sedgewick picked up on the importance of sidewalk cleanliness fairly early on in its history. In 1920, the village council passed a law that made it mandatory for every property owner to ensure that if they had a sidewalk in front of the building they owned, they would keep it clear from "all snow, ice, dirt or other obstructions." Even if the property owner didn't actually live on site, it was his or her responsibility to maintain that sidewalk. So if you were one of those rare individuals who owned a home, and rented it out, you had to make sure your tenant played nice and was willing to tackle any snow and debris. If that person didn't, you'd be the one in trouble, not your tenant. Talk about progressive thinking!

Nothing Noxious Here

If you think keeping your yard free from dandelions and couch grass is a nightmare, consider the tribulations our agricultural forefathers were under in 1922 when Alberta revamped its noxious weed statute:

☛ Landowners were expected to keep their property free of weeds, no matter how large that property was.

☛ As a landowner, you were also responsible for making sure no noxious weeds were "on the area between the boundaries of the said lands, and the centre line of all contiguous roads and road allowances."

☞ Inspectors could show up at any time to examine a property.

☞ If an inspector found weeds on your land, you had five days to destroy those weeds.

☞ Cutting weeds was not considered destroying them. If weeds weren't appropriately removed, an inspector could return, do the work and then charge the landowner for the trouble.

☞ Grain could not be sold if it contained "more than one seed of any noxious weed or weeds per ounce of such seed."

☞ Farmers couldn't even sell their grain for animal feed if "there [were] more than ten seeds of any noxious weed or weeds to every ounce of such grain."

Desired Methods of Disposal

It appears that putting "garbage, offal, dead animals, vegetable parings, ashes, cinders, rags, strings, hair combings, matches or any other matter or thing that would tend to obstruct any pipe or sewer in any water closet, bathtub, wash bowl, kitchen sink, or any other fixture connected with the sewer system of the town of Cochrane" was frowned upon in 1924. That's the year the town's council passed a bylaw providing the specifics on the appropriate use of Cochrane's sewer system. To ensure no one claimed ignorance of the matter, the bylaw further instructed residents to post a copy of the bylaw in a "clearly visible place in any bathroom or washing area." A fine of $50 could be issued to anyone neglecting any part of this bylaw, and if the offender didn't have money to pay the fine, he or she could end up spending as many as 21 days in jail—as soon as a local jail was built, that is.

Proper Packaging

I remember a time when my family was still allowed to burn garbage in a pile just a few yards away from our home. Ponoka put an end to this practice long before I was even a twinkle in my father's eye. In 1929, that town's council passed a law prohibiting the burning of garbage. It also legislated the kind of container residents must use to hold their garbage: the "refuse bucket" had to be zinc or galvanized steel and had to have a lid that sealed tightly. Ponoka's garbage collection process required residents to place their refuse buckets at the back of their properties for weekly pick up. Homes or businesses that didn't have an appropriate refuse bucket were provided with one by the town for a fee. Non-compliance would cost the offender a fine of $50 or up to 60 days in jail.

Garage Sale Etiquette

Anyone who has ever hosted a garage sale would agree it's a lot of work. But for the people living in Ponoka in 1939, a garage sale was even more time-consuming and demanded more of the seller than it does today. There was no quick set up and easy money to be made on your cast-offs. Instead, individuals hosting a garage sale were required to spend considerable time washing used clothing, polishing shoes and basically scrubbing the heck out of anything they planned to sell. This wasn't just as a courtesy to the potential buyers—it was law. The act declared that sale items were to be "disinfected by a method approved of by the local Board of Health." It's unclear how a bylaw officer would know whether someone hosting such a sale had used the approved method of cleaning, but if the bylaw officer declared the items unclean, the seller could receive a fine of up to $50.

Honouring our Dead

The last act of endearment we can perform for our loved ones once they pass is in how we lay them to rest. In 1954, Bowden's village council ensured everyone would receive a respectful, honourable burial through a set of regulations outlined in a new bylaw. Following a burial, excess earth was to be removed from the site. The bylaw also stated that "gravel, stone, paper or boxes or anything of a similar nature…be removed within 48 hours after the burial," and that "nothing of a size greater than one square inch be left in the vicinity of the grave."

The Cost of Growth

In 1968, Onoway was looking to expand its boundaries. To do so, it had to acquire additional lands. And so on April 8 of that year, the village council passed a bylaw to purchase the 25.69 acres comprising the "North East Quarter of Section 35-54-2-W5" from one Gordon Cust. The cost of this municipal growth was $2440.55, plus exchange. Although communities often annex property as their boundaries grow, it's hard to imagine that as recent as 1968, the cost of land was so very reasonable. Surely the cost of living is one more reason our seniors long for the "good old days."

Small, but Proud

In 2006, the village of Rosemary registered 388 residents according to Statistics Canada, but its size has never defined its stature. Good things come in small packages, as they say, and Rosemary is serious about putting its best foot forward in all areas. Going with the premise that beauty is as beauty does, on June 6, 1970, Rosemary's council passed a bylaw taking a firm stand to "regulate untidy and unsightly premises."

Property owners with accumulations of "dirty old implements or automobiles, iron, broken concrete pieces or other rubbish on any premises, so as to cause an untidy or unsightly condition, or a nuisance to such person being the owner, or the person entitled to the possession of the property upon which a nuisance is created, shall upon notification from the council and within the time limit specified within the said notice, cause the unsightly or untidy condition or nuisance to be moved or cleaned away."

Residents breaking this law were given notice to remedy the situation. And if they didn't, someone would do it for them and charge them for the service. These negligent landowners also had to pay a fine "not exceeding $100.00."

Turn Down the Volume

In 1997, Canmore outlawed noise, period. That's right, unless you are a town employee conducting noisy town business, no noise is allowed. Drive a vehicle with a noisy muffler and you could be slapped with a fine of $100 for the first offense, $500 for a second or subsequent offence, and if you're an extreme repeat offender and have annoyed the authorities enough, you could find yourself digging deep to pay a $2500 fine.

Even construction companies building or renovating in town had to ensure they had the appropriate "necessary federal, provincial

and municipal permits, licences and approvals" or they'd be in contravention of the noise bylaw. As well, construction work in this wilderness community could not take place before 7:00 AM or after 10:00 PM, Monday to Saturday. No construction of any kind is permitted on Sundays or statutory holidays.

No False Alarms

Residents in Red Deer must pay a $25 permit to the city before having an alarm installed in their home or business. If the alarm being installed made an audible sound when set off (I erroneously thought all alarms did this but apparently that is not the case), that alarm must silence itself within 15 minutes. Once an alarm has been set off, one of the keyholders responsible for that address must respond within 20 minutes—or else! And if the alarm bells ringing are determined to be a false alarm, the property owner will be charged $20 if it's a residential building, $40 for a small business of 500 square metres or less, and $60 for a large business. This bylaw was passed in 1968.

No Nuisance Here

In 2004, Falher passed its nuisance bylaw, and the councillors in that community made no bones about what was expected of area residents. Whereas some nuisance bylaws focus on noisy distractions such as too-loud parties, Falher's council created an almost all-encompassing bylaw. Noise is definitely a no-no, but so are unsightly weeds, grass that is too long and dandelions of any number.

There's no such thing as an uncontained compost pile in Falher—you can't pile your grass clippings beside the shed in this town. And if such a pile is hiding somewhere, and someone lets a town official know about it, the offender could be fined.

Although this all sounds reasonable and is nothing too out of the ordinary when compared to other communities, a couple of points in this bylaw are far less common:

☛ Residents can't allow the "accumulation of dirt, stones, old implements, automobiles, scrap iron or any other rubbish" to accumulate on their property—though it's hard to compare the unsightly quality of a rusted-out vehicle to a large pile of rocks.

☛ Falher residents also are forbidden to "permit the proliferation of, or harbour, any insect, animal, or other pest that is likely to spread disease, be destructive or dangerous, or otherwise become a nuisance." I'm just curious, but do teenagers count in this equation?

Anyone failing to comply with these regulations can be issued a written notice that the town isn't pleased and that the offender has seven days to deal with the problem. After that, the town could decide to fix the issue and charge the property owner.

Going Au Naturel

In 2004, the newly outlined land use bylaw in Cochrane required residents to practice "naturescaping" as defined by town council. That meant residents were encouraged to enhance their lots "through the use of natural indigenous vegetation, such as trees, shrubs, hedges, grasses, and other ground cover, in conjunction with permeable or pervious surfacing material, such as brick, stones, wood, and similar indigenous landscaping materials."

For single-dwelling homes, a minimum of 25 percent of the yard must follow this ground rule. Owners of multi-unit residential developments had to ensure 50 percent of their green space adhered to this guideline. And 100 percent of "all non-residential developments" were required to landscape their property following these regulations.

No Stone Unturned

In 2005, Grimshaw enacted legislation surrounding issues that some communities might label as "nuisances," but the town filed them under its "Community Standards" bylaw. Along with the usual references to eyesores and weeds gone wild, Grimshaw's council addressed everything possible. It wasn't just good enough to inform residents that they couldn't toss garbage on any "street, lane, sidewalk, parking lot, park or other public place." Council members in Grimshaw covered every possible scenario:

☞ Residents can't toss a "cardboard or wooden box, carton, container or receptacle of any kind" onto the aforementioned areas.

☞ Papers, wrappers, envelopes or coverings "of any kind whether paper or not" are also frowned upon.

☞ "Animal or vegetable matter or waste" isn't considered compost in this community, especially if you toss them into a back alley.

☞ Glass, crockery, nails, wires, electrical cords, metal, lumber, tires and bits and pieces of discarded and dismantled motorized vehicles are all considered rubbish and an eyesore, and if you have these items in your backyard, you are in contravention of this bylaw.

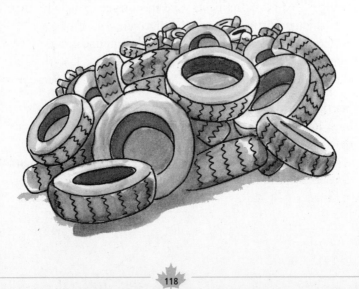

Eyesore or Art?

There are certain people who are quite proud of the "art" they create on dumpsters and lane-facing walls in the dark of night. But in Crossfield, this graffiti is an eyesore, not art, and isn't tolerated. According to that town's Graffiti Bylaw, passed on August 15, 2005, graffiti must be removed "within 120 hours after the graffiti has been reported," regardless if the graffiti is discovered on public or private property. If someone painted over a wall of your garage, it is up to you, the property owner, to pay to have the situation rectified. The town of Crossfield is responsible for covering graffiti found on public property. And you can't use just any method to remove the offending eyesore. The graffiti is to be removed "using the most environmentally safe method possible."

Reduce, Reuse, Recycle

Out of a concern for growing landfills and the need for environmental stewardship, Cochrane enacted a new waste management bylaw in December 2005. Regardless the size of family, each residence had a "two unit limit" for their curbside garbage. These "units" of waste are defined as "a plastic garbage bag up to 66 cm x 91 cm (26 inch x 36 inch), or one waste container with a volume no greater than 80 litres (20 gallons), and shall not weigh more than 15 kilograms (33 pounds)." If your trash bag is even slightly larger than these measurements, it automatically counts as two units and residents are charged accordingly.

Garbage Is Garbage

So much for the old adage that one man's trash is another man's treasure. It is against the law to "scavenge waste from a waste container, plastic garbage bag or a commercial bin" in Cochrane according to that community's 2005 waste management bylaw.

Save the Trees

I imagine that someone, at some time, hiked along the ditches or entered a city park in Cold Lake with an axe and had a purpose in mind—to cut down a tree. Why else, I ask myself, would the city council find it necessary to enact that community's 2005 tree bylaw, forbidding people from removing "a public tree or [causing] a public tree to be removed from any public lands"? And that's not all! Regulations surrounding "public trees on public lands" in Cold Lake are quite extensive:

☛ Only city staff can plant "public" trees, unless a resident has acquired "written authorization from the Parks Foreman" to do so.

☛ You can't tear bark off public trees or "cause the bark of a public tree to be removed," without permission.

☛ Individuals can't "use or cause the use of an object of any kind to penetrate the bark of a public tree," which means young lovers in Cold Lake have to find other ways to declare their undying love instead of carving their initials into the old oak down the lane.

☛ You can't attach a sign or poster, an electrical cord, or anything else, on a public tree.

☛ And finally, "No person shall place any building materials or other similar object against a public tree without…"—you've got it—"prior written authorization from the Parks Foreman."

Government Generosity

Not every community might be able to access financial help from their local governments, but at least one organization in Hanna managed to loosen the town's purse strings. But maybe it had something to do with what the councillors in 2006 liked to do on their time off. That's the year the Hanna Golf and Country Club/Hanna Municipal Golf Course Association approached their town fathers for a $50,000 loan to expand the course to 18 holes. The money was drawn from the town's general reserve fund.

This "2006 Golf Course Loan Bylaw" appears to have been an interest-free project because the repayment conditions included in the document make mention of repayment to be made "in five (5) equal payments of $10,000 commencing in 2007, unless Community Facility Enhancement Program funding is obtained in 2007 sufficient to pay the entire loan."

Skating on a New Rink

Of course, providing some kind of financial assistance to community endeavours isn't all that out of the ordinary. Take Marwayne, for example. On April 19, 1962, the council in this northeast community passed a bylaw "concerning a Grant to assist in financing the Skating Rink."

The amount of money "granted" was considerably smaller than Hanna's, mind you. Marwayne offered $150 to "assist in the financing of the Skating Rink." This bylaw certainly speaks loudly to the increase in the cost of living over the years!

From this Day Forward

Never having purchased a burial plot to this point in my life, it was a surprise to me that the Cemetery Plot/Niche Deed as outlined by Drumheller's 2009 cemetery bylaw includes the clause "To Have and to Hold...forever." Once you purchase such a deed in this town, the contract appears to be more difficult to extract yourself from than the marriage vows the clause echoes.

The only time this deed can be taken over by someone else is if it is transferred to another family member, and then, only on approval of the town council.

If that doesn't work, and you really don't want to spend all of eternity overlooking the hoodoos, you can request the town buy the plot back—but it could cost you. Should the town decide the plot is something they can resell, they may purchase the plot back at 85 percent of its market value "at the date of resale." That means if prices went up, you might get your initial investment back. If prices decreased, you'll be out of pocket at least some of the money you spent—if the town agrees to the buy back the plot at all.

That the plot you purchased could theoretically be "deemed unusable by the Town for any reason," which to my way of thinking suggests that same "unusable" designation could be applied to a plot that is currently in use, is more than unsettling—pardon the pun. I can imagine the fallout from flash floodwaters or random earthquakes unearthing long-passed ancestors.

Aside from that, it's clear that if you're married and you and your spouse want to purchase neighbouring plots, don't let your emotions rule. An ugly divorce or a change of heart down the road could end up costing you more than you'd expected.

Concerning Compost...

Stavely's town council is quite strict about how its residents must dispose of composting materials and what can be considered as such. In 2008, Stavely passed Bylaw 736, also known as the Community Standards Bylaw. While it seems clear to me that the following items are not considered composting materials, the bylaw creators felt a need to explain to residents that they are not allowed to put "cat feces, dog feces, animal parts or animal

meat on a composting pile or in a composting container."
Furthermore, compost piles or containers designed for
composting materials can't be kept closer than 10 metres to any
home, they must be free from any "offensive odours" and must
not attract pests.

Shhh—I'm Sleeping

You might be a morning person, but if you live in Stavely and
plan on getting a head start on the chores around the house and
are ready to roll before 7:00 AM, you'll have to tackle the quiet
jobs first. It is against the law in that town to operate a "power
lawn mower, power snow removal equipment or motorized model
aircraft" between 11:00 PM and 7:00 AM.

A Loving Approach to Lawns

Unsightly weeds that threaten to run rampant on neighbouring
properties are frowned upon in Drumheller. That town's weed
control bylaw dictates the course of actions residents must take in
order to eradicate any weed problem they might have on their
property.

Taking an environmentally friendly approach to begin with,
property owners are encouraged to "mow, hand pull or hoe
weeds" that they discover on their property. If that doesn't work,
"talk to a gardening expert." And as a last resort, "consider using
herbicides." In any case, residents who allow the "uncontrolled
growth of grass and plants to the point where they become
unsightly, form a nuisance, are not controlled or managed or
cause a fire hazard" can find themselves facing a fine—or an
onslaught of professionals descending on their property to fix the
problem and then providing them with a bill for their services.

Legalities in Legal

Along with keeping the noise level down during sleeping hours, the folks in Legal have to pay attention to the lights they've got shining around their home, according to that town's nuisance bylaw. Section seven of that bit of legislation states that:

☛ "No owner or occupier of a property shall allow an outdoor light to shine directly into the living or sleeping area of an adjacent dwelling house."

☛ No one could have a light that would "…shine in a manner in which it will interfere with the effectiveness of a traffic control device…" or "…will interfere with an operator of a motor vehicle, a pedestrian or any proper user of a highway."

I don't know about you, but this bylaw has me wondering what kind of situation propelled the need for these explicit rules?

THAT OUGHTA BE A LAW

Although Cochrane has yet to make this innovative environmentally friendly practice a law, the town's administration never tires of encouraging its residents to do so. Since 2008, the town has suggested that its residents collect potable water in rain barrels. Families interested in doing so can order the barrels from the Cochrane Environmental Action Committee during the town's Saturday morning Farmers' Market. According to the town's "Water Conservation Strategy," "some folks with one or more rain barrels don't put a drop of municipal water on their properties all summer!" Sounds like a brilliant water conservation option that should be a law.

OUTHOUSES

If you've ever spent time in the bush, you'll know what it means to "adapt" to your surroundings when it comes to dealing with natural bodily functions. But even on these occasions there are rules of etiquette, if you will, on how to best deal with the matter of human waste in an environmentally friendly way. Find a secluded area where someone might not show up shortly, pitch a tent and take with you a small trowel, a couple of plastic bags and a "small nylon sack to carry these items." There's more on this, but I think you get the idea.

If relieving yourself in the woods is this complicated, it's no wonder the issue of water closets, outhouses and indoor plumbing were given serious thought, and pretty uniformly really, by community councils across Alberta.

Potty Problems

In 1916, officers in Peace River could impose fines of up to $100 for anyone who didn't follow the exact specifications when it came to building an outhouse in town. At that time, outdoor water closets couldn't be placed closer than eight metres from "any street line of the village." These outhouses had to have a "hinged trap or door in the rear thereof in such manner as shall provide free access to any village scavenger."

By 1920, these guidelines clearly weren't detailed enough, or perhaps individuals weren't bothering to build an outhouse at all and merely squatted in the bushes to do their business because the earlier bylaw was repealed and another enacted in its place.

The newer bylaw stated that anyone building, living in or maintaining a "house, shack, tent or other erection whatsoever used as a dwelling place within the Town of Peace River" had to first build a privy. The 25-foot (eight-metre) restriction from any street line remained in effect, as did the "tightly fitting hinged trap or door" required in the rear to clean it out. This bylaw also explained that the privy had to be "tight and flyproof," sport a "tightly fitting cover over the seat" and have a "ventilator of dimensions not less than four (4) inches square leading from underneath the seat of the Privy or Closet to the outside…" The $100 fine for non-compliance remained, along with court costs. Neglecting to pay the piper could cost the offender up to 60 days in jail, "with or without hard labour."

The Pits

The town of Okotoks developed regulations on the building of local outhouses as early as 1910. A bylaw issued that year made it mandatory for residents to abandon the practice of building dirt outhouses and to outfit their privies with metal pails. Lucy Rowed, historical assistant with the town of Okotoks Museum and Archives, explained that the town hired a "Scavenger."

It was the duty of this individual to "empty unmaintained, over-flowing or stinky closets at a cost to the owner of 25 cents per pail." The bylaw doesn't specify how much this poor soul received as a wage for doing this chore.

No Privies Allowed

Founded in 1892, Crossfield showed itself as a forward-thinking community right from the beginning. Out of concern for the health and welfare of its residents, the village council enacted its "Bylaw for the prevention of disease, etc." in 1913:

☞ The first order of business in this bylaw was to outlaw "privy pits" within village limits.

☞ Water-tight "dry earth or chemical closets" were allowed, but their construction had to be approved by council, and residents were required to use "a necessary quantity of absorbent or chemical."

☛ Cesspools had to be constructed of "concrete or brick lined with cement so as to be non-porous and to be properly ventilated."

☛ Between April 1 and November 1 of each year, residents were responsible for emptying and cleaning these "closets and cesspools" twice a month. During the remainder of the year, this lovely job was relegated to a monthly task.

☛ And finally addressing the "etc." part of the bylaw, "All garbage, swill, slops, shall be placed in water-tight receptacles with tight fitting covers and removed regularly once a week between the first day of May and the first day of November in each year."

Standards for Sanitation

Rooming houses, restaurants, hotels, laundries and boarding houses had a big renovation project on their hands in Peace River in 1919. On August 18 of that year, the village council passed a bylaw requiring these businesses to construct a concrete cesspit "in such a manner as may be approved by the Health Officer of the Village or of any other officer or agent of the Village who may be authorized by the Council to approve of such cesspits."

Minimizing Odours

Westlock's village council strictly regulated the distance between a home and its outhouse in 1946. That was the year the council passed a bylaw outlining the following requirements:

☛ An outhouse couldn't be located any closer to the rear property line than five feet (1.5 metres).

☛ The outhouse had to be a minimum of two feet (60 centimetres) from a lane or adjoining lot.

☛ Outhouses couldn't be located any closer than 50 feet (15 metres) from a well.

☛ There had to be a minimum of 20 feet (six metres) between an outhouse and any "dwelling, store, restaurant or any other place where food is stored or consumed."

Proper Materials

Ponoka was equally tough about the erection of outhouses in its community. In 1929, every home or public building was required to have an outhouse, and building guidelines for these outhouses were strictly enforced.

The seat of an outhouse had to be "securely attached to the framework of the outhouse in such a manner that same may be easily and expeditiously lifted up and left standing open when required." Dugout pits were no longer acceptable, and anyone with that kind of outhouse had to dismantle it and cover in

the pit. Galvanized buckets were to be used as receptacles instead of dug pits. Residents had to remove the buckets twice a month and dump their contents in the designated spot in the town's nuisance grounds.

Tardy residents putting off the reconstruction of their existing, non-compliant outhouses could find town workers on their property doing the job—and charging the resident and/or landowner a hefty sum for doing it, as well as a $50 fine and/or as many as 60 days behind bars "with or without hard labour."

Outlawing the Outhouse

Speaking of privies, Barrhead made it a little more difficult for anyone with a sudden and unmanageable need to relieve oneself. In 1970, Barrhead's town council passed a bylaw outlawing outhouses on private properties—or at least those within town limits, and even those located on properties "bordering town streets where sewer and water mains were located." Homes within this catchment area had to have workable washrooms that were properly connected to the town's sewer system.

Anyone living in this area with an outhouse on their property had 30 days to remove the offending structure and fill in the pit. Homes with outhouses still standing after the 30-day grace period could find city workers doing the "dirty work" for them. This might seem like a charitable gesture, until these homeowners received their next property tax bill and noticed the fee for the service included in the amount owed.

The Perfect Pit

Add water to one part Portland Cement and seven parts of gravel and clean sand, with no rocks having a diameter larger than two inches, and you should have the perfect mix to construct a privy pit in Hardisty in 1911. That was the year town council amended the bylaw to include a clause on the proper construction of outhouses in their community. And to ensure these criteria were followed to the letter, the "whole work and material" of all newly constructed pits had to be inspected and approved "before being passed for use."

Furred, Featured and Other Creatures

Man is the only creature that consumes without producing. He does not give milk, he does not lay eggs, he is too weak to pull the plough, he cannot run fast enough to catch rabbits. Yet he is lord of all the animals.

–George Orwell, *Animal Farm*

ANIMAL CONTROL

Not all that long ago it was fairly common for people to pen a few chickens in their backyard. Add a pig or two, along with a substantial vegetable garden, and a family was set for their year's worth of sustenance. In fact, some rural communities still have the odd resident who is bent on maintaining the practice.

But as communities grew and neighbours got closer, the unsightly sounds of livestock snorting and groaning, and the smell of the occasionally overpacked chicken coop, caused some measure of discomfort for neighbours who weren't agriculturally inclined. In time, it seemed necessary to contain the problem by imposing rules and regulations if neighbours were going to remain neighbourly to one another.

The evolution of livestock bylaws makes for interesting reading, and in many instances includes the expected treatment of wild species, but the bylaws associated with household pets are equally interesting. Domestic animals, like cats or dogs and the odd exotic creature, make up the majority of today's animal control bylaws. And yet the issues around domestic animals are not all that different than those surrounding farm animals. No one wants the neighbour's cat using our flowerbed as a litter box— they leave behind an unsightly mess and acrid aroma. And heaven help me if I ever find a boa slithering through my lawn or in my basement because it has escaped the confines of its master's house!

Beasts of the Prairie

While this province's first inhabitants revered the buffalo, it appears not all new settlers extended the same respect to this majestic species. On March 22, 1877, concern for the preservation and protection of the buffalo resulted in the lieutenant-governor of the North-West Territories enacting an ordinance on the issue. Included in the document were the following restrictions:

☞ "No pound, pit, or like enclosure or contrivance shall, at any time, be formed or used in the North-West Territories, for the capture of buffalo."

☞ A buffalo could not be killed by running it into a river or lake or over a steep cliff.

☞ If you were hunting buffalo, you had to be serious in your intentions. Tracking them down and killing them just "from the mere motive of amusement, or wanton destruction, or solely to secure their tongues, choice cuts, or peltries" was against the law— a hunter had to use at least "one half of the flesh of a buffalo."

☞ No one was allowed to hunt female buffalo between November 15 and the following August 14.

☞ "Indians and non-Treaty Indians" were exempt from the ban on hunting female buffalo between November 15 and the following February 14.

☛ A traveller in dire need of sustenance, or a starving squatter dying from starvation, could kill a buffalo "to satisfy his immediate wants."

This ordinance was repealed on August 2, 1878. But I would wager that if cowboy ran one of these majestic beasts off a steep cliff somewhere or conducted some other nasty behaviour against them today, he'd find himself up against the strong arm of the law!

Hold Your Horses!

If you owned a stallion that was a year or older in 1878 and it escaped your custody, you'd be in hot water unless you made haste to get it back. According to "An Ordinance respecting Stallions," passed on August 2, 1878, in what was then the North-West Territories, owners who didn't pick up their truant charges were fined five dollars outright, and another "twenty-five cents per day for the keep of the said horse every day it has been in...custody." If the owner didn't cough up the cash to cover the fine, he could be hauled into court and face another $20 fine plus court costs. If he still didn't pay up, the negligent owner could have his property sold and the proceeds used to settle his accounts.

A Deadly Situation

Back in the day, poisons like strychnine were the weapon of choice for destroying pesky wildlife that were interfering with domestic animals and livestock. Of course, poisons aren't partial—they can kill cows and horses too. So on August 2, 1878, the North-West Territories council passed "An Ordinance respecting Poisons" in order to define how poisons could be administered and the safest ways for residents to apply them.

Residents couldn't use poison for the "purpose of capturing or destroying any animal"—because poison could be used against wildlife, you have to assume this point refers to domestic animals.

If it was deemed in the public interest by a "Stipendiary Magistrate or Justice of the Peace," poison could be used "for a period not exceeding three months…between sunset and sunrise, at not more than ten places, other than on a public road or trail, inside of a radius of ten miles from his own residence or other place specially named in the license, for the purpose of destroying such wild animals." No mention is made about what might happen if the neighbour's dog died as a result of happening along one of the approved poisoning sites.

Bridle Your Beasts

In 1908, the municipal council of Lloydminster passed a bylaw stating animal owners "or any person having the custody or care of any horse, mule, jack, cattle, sheep, goat, swine, rabbit, goose, turkey, duck or poultry" must keep control of their animals when passing along community streets. Perhaps it was because livestock were a little more unruly than domestic dogs and cats that they were singled out. Either way, farmers who lost control of their herd of cattle could be slapped with a $20 fine or up to seven days in jail. This is completely understandable, but how you could manage to walk your goose down Main Street and ensure it didn't dash off to peck a passerby escapes me. I'd say it was probably safer to leave the critter at home.

Pen Your Poultry

The town of Hardisty must have had a problem with feathered livestock running willy-nilly throughout the community since the issue of flighty fowl made its first appearance in May 1911. Bylaw number six stated that, "no person or persons shall permit any chickens, turkeys, geese or ducks to run at large within the limits of the said Town of Hardisty." The reason for the bylaw was simple—these critters caused untold damage to "gardens, flower beds, or shrubberies" belonging to Hardisty residents. If your chicken was caught gallivanting through town, you'd face a fine of between one and five dollars, which was likely more than the chicken was worth back then.

From Poultry to Pig Pens

Farmers or residents keeping pigpens, cow pens, sheds or stables within Hardisty's town limits were expected to keep their property clean. Should anyone complain about offensive odours, general uncleanliness or outright neglect, the offending animal owner could be "fined for each day of keeping and maintaining the same in offensive condition, any sum not less than One Dollar ($1.00) nor more than Ten Dollars ($10.00)." This bylaw was passed in 1911.

Two Pig Limit

Lloydminster's village council came up with a compromise when it came to residents keeping pigs within town limits. In an effort to minimize odour and ensure cleanliness and control of the situation, the council passed a bylaw in 1918 limiting the number of pigs any family could keep in town to two. The pigs also had to have proper housing, which could be located no closer than "100 feet from any dwelling." After two years of trying to maintain the compromise, council reassessed the situation and decided it wasn't working out as well as they'd hoped. The bylaw was repealed, and residents could no longer keep pigs on their property within town limits.

Pig Pens and Offensive Odours

Ponoka curtailed any problem with pigs it sensed were stewing as early as 1914. Although the town council didn't outright ban the animals from town, it did set up fairly strict guidelines about how owners should care for their animals to limit any discomfort for their neighbours. Anyone wanting to keep pigs on their property had to ensure the pens were built a minimum of 300 feet (91.5 metres) from homes or businesses, and "no more than two pigs of any one age shall be kept in any one pen." Owners were expected to keep their swine pens "dry and free from offensive odours," and if your neighbour complained that you weren't doing an appropriate job in this matter, you could find yourself facing off with local officials.

Pack up Your Pigs

On April 30, 1921, Beiseker enacted a bylaw prohibiting residents from keeping hogs of "any kind or age" within village limits. According to the bylaw, anyone who at that time had pigs on their property had to find homes for their swine elsewhere by May 15 of the same year. Interestingly enough, there is no mention of a fine or penalty should residents refuse to follow through with the new legislation. Fowl, it seems, got a bit of a reprieve for a time. A bylaw passed that same day allowed residents to keep chickens and other feathered creatures on town property provided they were kept in a safe and secure enclosure, and their pens met the sanitation standards of a health inspector.

No Second Chances

Residents of Peace River were expected to keep their pet "dog or bitch" under control at all times. If they were found "running at large," they could be "forthwith destroyed by any Police Officer or License Inspector of the Town, or may be dealt with or disposed of in manner hereinafter provided." This motion was made law on May 10, 1920. Residents had no second chance when it came to their pooch running loose.

Service Providers

Even though motorized vehicles were becoming more and more popular by 1921, most rural folks still relied on their horses and gear to get around. Acquiring a good horse meant searching out a mare and stallion with good lineage before encouraging the coupling that would eventually produce a foal. That year, the provincial government outlined a statute entitled "Stallion Enrolment" that outlined the exact manner with which stallion owners could charge or receive fees for service:

☛ Stallions brought into the province to provide stud services had to have their credentials listed in the Stallion Enrolment.

☛ To qualify for inclusion in this elite list, owners had to provide all "such evidence as it may require regarding the breeding, ownership, soundness, and freedom from hereditary, infectious, contagious, or transmissible disease of such stallion."

☛ Prior to enrolment, a government-appointed official inspected every inch of the stallion in question, reporting every "grave defect of conformation in any such stallion, and (if such there be) any bone-spavin, bog-spavin, ring-bone, side-bone, or curb, apparently due to defective conformation of structural weakness, and any cataract, amaurosis, periodic opthalmia (moon-blindness), laryngeal hemiplegia (roaring or whistling) chorea (spring-halt) or St. Vitus' Dance, or any other condition rendering it in the judgment of the inspector unfit for breeding purposes."

☞ Enrolment only lasted until January 1 of each year. At that time, a new application had to be completed.

☞ Stallions were inspected at least every three years until they were nine.

☞ Detailed performance reports were expected by the authorities on a regular basis, including the number of mares that were "in foal" following the stallion's services. Should that number be lower than acceptable—the acceptable number of pregnancies per performance were not detailed in this statute—"the chairman may…cancel the certificate of enrolment previously issued in respect of such stallion."

Talk about an unnerving performance evaluation!

Your Loss, My Gain

The village of Beiseker, located northeast of Calgary, took a unique stand when it came to horses and cattle running at large within their community boundaries. According to a bylaw passed in April 1921, "any animal found at large or trespassing upon any lands or premises enclosed by a lawful fence, contrary to the provisions of this By-Law, shall be liable to be impounded and sold according to the provisions of this By-Law unless the charges, expenses, and fees be sooner paid." In other words, the owner's loss could very well result in an increase in the town coffers.

Punishments for Cruelty

While Beiseker's residents might not have wanted to share their living space with stinky, noisy farm animals, they also weren't in favour of undue and harsh treatment of their furry and feathered friends—and they were very explicit about it. You have to wonder what kind of incident led to the passing of that community's bylaw to prevent cruelty to animals. In particular, the 1921 bylaw states that no one could "wantonly, cruelly or unnecessarily beat, bind, ill-treat, abuse, overdrive or torture any cattle, poultry, dog or other domestic animal or bird."

Furthermore, bystanders witnessing such ill treatment were forbidden from encouraging, aiding or assisting "at the fighting or beating of any kind of animals, whether of domestic or wild nature." Anyone found mistreating an animal or watching it being mistreated without intervening on its behalf was hauled up in front of the justice of the peace to learn his or her fate.

Tightening the Reins

By 1924, Beiseker's council took an even tougher stand on the issue of animals in town. In July of that year, the authorities made it illegal for anyone to "tether any animals or animal of any kind, within Block One and Block Two, Plan 40IIX, Beiseker, or any other place in the said Village where such animals would be creating a public nuisance."

Given these guidelines, ordinary citizens probably had no clear understanding of where, if anywhere, they could lawfully tether their animals. Regardless, it appears residents couldn't plead ignorance on the matter. If they misunderstood, and subsequently broke the law, it would cost them between $10 and $25.

Wandering Not Allowed—Anywhere

In 1922, Alberta revamped its Domestic Animals statutes, leaving no doubt about the definition of the term "at large." Leaving nothing to chance, the statute explains that "no mischievous animal," "no prohibited animal" and no animal of any kind was allowed to wander about unsupervised anywhere in the province. In fact, a herd of cattle could be considered "running at large" unless there were a "sufficient number of herders to ensure the easy retention of immediate, continuous and effective control over each animal comprised in the same."

No Goosing Around

The folks down in Falher pulled the reins on their livestock by 1935. That was the year they enacted a bylaw making it illegal for any farm animal, including "horse, mule, ass, cattle, sheep, pig, goat or goose," to run about throughout village streets. Animals were to be "securely tethered" on their keeper's property, or under "immediate, continuous and effective control" of their owners.

Late Bloomers

It appears residents in the now, ever-growing city of Airdrie didn't make too much of a fuss about livestock within their community's limits until 1952. That's when a bylaw came into effect making it illegal to keep livestock within village limits. Dogs, cats, parrots and canaries were exempt from this ban on animals, "providing the council [did] not consider them objectionable." There were exceptions to this rule, but animal owners had to approach council for special permission in order to contravene the law. Even with that initial approval, the issue didn't end there. These same people had to reapply for permission annually, and council might change their minds about the initially agreed upon arrangement. By 1968, there was no longer any recourse for residents who wanted to keep livestock within town limits. A bylaw passed that year made it illegal to keep any "horses, cattle or chickens" in Airdrie. Perhaps pigs weren't ever an issue since the bylaw does not directly mention the curly-tailed porkers.

Putting a Lid on Dairy

Don't ask me why, but Cochrane had to deal with a number of complaints coming through the area's health inspector back in 1941. It appears residents suddenly realized a dairy barn was operating within village limits—you would think such an obvious operation was hard to miss—and it was causing some concern among neighbours. They didn't appreciate the sights, sounds and smells of dairy cattle mulling about, though they no doubt enjoyed the milk, cream and butter the animals produced. Once the concern was brought to council, along with the "adverse report of the Health Inspector...and in the interest of the health of the community," council members decided that "the operating of dairy barns and the keeping of milch [sic] cows within the Village limits be no longer permitted."

Embracing the Rural Roots

The residents of Fort Saskatchewan haven't forgotten their agricultural heritage. In fact, they've embraced it in a unique way as recently as 2002. That's when the city council passed a bylaw making it legal for herding dogs to move about freely while minding a herd of sheep. That dogs can wander about freely might seem surprising to some, but it makes perfect sense when you consider that Fort Saskatchewan still has pasturing areas in the city where sheep roam about freely. Since it's unreasonable for a farmer to follow the herd day in and day out, a herding dog is a necessary tool in managing the woolly throng, hence the adoption of the 2002 bylaw.

Going to the Birds

Here's a story about a story behind a bylaw, after the fact.

According to Tina Williamson-Ward, management assistant with the town of Three Hills, folks wanting to keep chickens in town need to have approval from council first. On February 22, 1999, Three Hills council passed its animal control bylaw regulating all animals, including dogs, cats, hamsters, rabbits, gerbils, domestic mice, budgies, parakeets, cockatiels, anything defined as "wildlife" in the Wildlife Act and any "other animal which at the discretion of the Animal Control Officer is generally and widely accepted as a domestic pet."

It appears that chickens fall into this general category under the definition of "fowl," and since it's a no-no to let your "pets" or other animals roam about freely, keeping chickens loose on your lawn might pose a problem—especially if they slip through the fence and run amok on town streets.

If you're wondering why chickens need to be mentioned at all, just hear me out. Williamson-Ward explained that some residents have asked for permission to keep chickens "for lawn care." She explained that, "apparently some people have a contraption that they put the chicken in and the chicken then eats the lawn." Other residents have asked to keep a goat for the same purpose—which in my opinion makes more sense because goats make less of a mess.

This story brings to mind the time the administration of a church camp I was employed at hauled two sheep in a fishing boat to our little island paradise to let them roam free for the summer. The idea was similar—they'd keep the grass down and, by default, minimize the mosquito population. It worked too. As an added bonus for the sheep farmer, the two sheep gained a significant amount of weight and avoided becoming a bear's lunch. The farmer was quite happy when his sheep were returned, plump and ready for slaughter. It seems this loaning out of livestock as a living, breathing, mowing machine is obviously not as unusual as I once thought.

In any case, residents in Three Hills can, coincidentally, keep as many as three chickens, or "fowl," on their property. However, neighbours "on all sides" of that individual's property have to agree to the idea, and the chickens and yard have to be kept clean. Personally, I'm thinking it would be easier to keep the lawn clean sans chickens, but that's another story.

Oh, and one more interesting point to this chicken story—anyone keeping chickens in this community cannot decide to eat them later!

PETS AND OTHER COMPANIONS

Judging by the number of people I've known over the years who've thumbed their nose at community bylaws requiring the licensing of pets, it came as quite a surprise to me that this kind of bylaw has been around for quite some time. Municipalities were punishing pet owners for allowing their dogs to wander almost as soon as these legislative bodies were formed.

What is most interesting about the bylaws surrounding pets and the responsibilities of pet owners is the wording of some of these bylaws, the reasons why some of them were formed in the first place and the extent of responsibility officials were given to ensure these laws were followed to the letter.

Extreme Measures

A dog might be man's best friend, but as early as 1907, the residents of Cardston had to prove their loyalties if they wanted to keep their pooch. In 1901, almost immediately after the town was incorporated, residents had to pay a licence fee to keep a dog. But there must have been a number of truant dog owners in town because in 1907 the earlier bylaw was repealed, and a tougher law was enacted in its place. Bylaw 98 came down hard on dog owners who didn't pay their licence fees of "two dollars for each dog and five dollars for each bitch." A town official was responsible for ensuring every dog in the community was licensed. Dogs found without the appropriate licences were returned to their owners with the full expectation that the fee would be "paid on demand." If that didn't happen, the town official was granted the power to "cause such dog or bitch to be forthwith destroyed." This kind of law wouldn't go over without a lot of opposition these days.

Pardon the Short Notice

At their January 23, 1911, meeting, members of Airdrie's village council passed a bylaw requiring dog owners to license their mutts within one month of acquiring the dog or it would be shot. You would presume residents who already had dogs at the time of the creation of the bylaw also had a month to purchase a licence.

Keeping Tabs on the Pet Population

In July 1912, Coronation not only had a bylaw in place to deal with the "taxation of dogs and restraining the running at large" of these critters, but it also had already amended the bylaw. By this point in the community's history, dog owners within town limits were expected to license their animals: two dollars for a dog and three for a bitch. The town then added the requirement of including information on the dog owner, the breed of dog, its name and its description.

At a predetermined time every year, Coronation police officers, or someone else appointed to the task, had to ensure every dog in town was tagged. It was the "duty" of these officials to scope out wayward dogs, find their masters and "immediately notify every person reported to him as the owner of an unregistered dog in Town, and require such owner forthwith to register the same and comply with the requirements of this by-law." Owners who hadn't paid their dues were "sued" five dollars. And any "bitch in heat" found roaming about would be "destroyed by the police officers or other persons appointed to carry out the provisions by this by-law by the Council."

The Birds Have It

If a cat was your pet of choice and you owned one in Fort Saskatchewan back in 1938, there were a few unique laws you were expected to follow. Cats had to wear bells on their collars—and yes, this was legislated. If your cat was discovered gallivanting about without one, it was deemed "an enemy to the Song Birds." The cat owner, if known, could face a $10 fine or a week in the "nearest common Gaol." Worse still, the cat could be shot and killed by the authorities. Why, you ask? The answer is quite simple really. The folks in Fort Saskatchewan loved their songbirds, and everyone knows cats are also quite fond of the feathered creatures—and not in a cuddly, loving kind of way.

Put a bell on a cat's collar and any bird a feline might be trying to sneak up on would get fair warning that a predator was nearby. This innovative, if not slightly biased law, was on the books until 1958 before the council of the day saw fit to have it repealed.

The Birds Have It, Take Two

Fort Saskatchewan residents weren't the only ones concerned about their songbirds. Also in 1938, the town of Stavely, located off Highway 2, midway between Calgary and Lethbridge, enacted a cat-belling bylaw. Residents hollered so loud and long that the town was "the first community in the world" to enact this kind of law. Their motivation for pursuing this action was in response to concerns voiced by the Audubon Society, which had announced that domestic cats were killing large populations of songbirds. Cats without bells in Stavely were also in danger of being shot and killed. The town council even hired a man named Halvar "Red" Rostrum to "shoot every cat or kitten he found wandering about without a bell—as long as they were shot before noon." Not sure where the "before noon" part came from.

Late Bloomers?

It wasn't until June 10, 1980, that Blackfalds enacted a bylaw dealing with the "harbouring of any wild or domestic animals or poultry." Bylaw 462 prohibited residents from keeping "wild or domestic animals or poultry, in any areas within the corporate limits of the Town of Blackfalds, excepting where the property is assessed as agricultural land use or [on] a parcel of land which is over three acres." We can only presume dogs and cats were exempt from this bylaw, but because they aren't mentioned directly, it certainly leaves one wondering.

Proper Burial

Pet owners in Three Hills are required to take their responsibilities seriously during their pet's life—and after it dies.

Properly disposing of a deceased pet is quite a serious matter in this community. The animal control bylaw requires any dead animal to be "disposed of within 48 hours." Tossing it in a BFI bin isn't good enough either, not that I would ever advocate such a thing. Instead, the pet must be "buried with a covering of at least 4 feet of earth," and the grave "must be immediately filled in" as soon as it has been dug.

Taking a Tougher Stand

Blackfalds' most recent animal bylaw was enacted on November 27, 2007. The lengthy legislation suggests the town council has taken a tougher stand on animal control than they might have decades ago:

☛ Animal licence fees are due by January 31 of each year. New pet owners are allowed 30 days' grace to acquire the licence, and licensed animals must wear an identification tag at all times.

☛ Owners of cats seen to be "stalking birds" can be fined.

☛ If your dog "barks or howls so as to disturb a person," you could be feeding the town coffers.

☛ Unless you owned a menagerie of critters before this bylaw came into effect, you are limited to owning no more than two dogs or three cats.

☛ If you own more than the allotted maximum for cats or dogs, you need to acquire a "kennel or cattery licence."

☛ Residents with unaltered female cats or dogs are required to keep them "housed and confined during the whole period [they are] in heat." Once again, the males get off scot-free!

☛ Residents owning what town officials label as "restricted or threatening dogs" are required to keep that animal "securely confined indoors or in a locked pen capable of preventing the entry of another person besides the owner." This begs the question: how humane is it for anyone in this community to own such an animal?

And finally, if your cat has defecated on or damaged another person's property, the affronted resident is well within his or her right to acquire a stray cat or skunk trap. Traps are available from the "office of the Contractor" for a $10 fee, plus a $20 deposit to ensure the trap is returned. The complainant is responsible for checking the trap as often as the contractor deemed necessary. Once an animal is trapped, it must be delivered back to the town office for the animal control officer to deal with or picked up by the owner within 24 hours. Here are a few rules that residents bent on trapping their neighbour's cat must follow:

☛ The trap must be placed in a shaded area.

☛ The trap must not be set up when "temperatures are consistently below (0) degrees Celsius."

☛ The trapped animal should be treated with gentleness.

☛ It is absolutely forbidden to tease, poke or be generally disagreeable to the trapped animal. Folks found guilty of abusing a trapped animal could be charged "under section 446 of the Criminal Code of Canada."

Reading the Riot Act

Talk about covering all of your bases! Taber left nothing to chance when it created its Exotic and Wild Animal Bylaw. In 2007, the town made it illegal for residents to keep a pet the administration deemed as exotic—and when they wrote out the details, almost every species known to man was listed.

According to the bylaw, no one living within the "corporate limits of the town of Taber" could own any of the following:

☛ "marsupials or pouched mammals—kangaroos, American opossums, marsupial wolf, Tasmanian devil, Tasmanian tiger, pouched mouse, Australian bandicoot...pouched rat, koala, cuscus (a marsupial monkey), flying phalanger (similar to a flying squirrel), wombat

☛ "carnivorous land mammals—wolf, coyote, fox, wild dog, bear, raccoon, panda, coatimundi, weasels, stoat, wolverine, marten, mink, badger, skunk, otter, mongoose, civet, genet, hyena, ocelot, lion, tiger, leopard, panther, lynx, mountain lion, bobcat, seals, sea lions, walruses, bats

☛ "odd-toed hoofed animals—horse, ass, zebra, mule, donkeys, tapir, rhinoceros

☛ "even-toed hoofed animals—all pigs, warthogs (excluding Vietnamese pot-bellied pigs), peccaries, hippopotamus, camel, dromedaries, llama, alpacas, mouse deer, deer, reindeer, caribou, moose, elk, antelope, giraffe, okapi, pronged-horned antelope, sheep, goat, bison, water buffalo, musk ox, cow, heifer, steer, bull, anteaters, sloths, armadillos, elephants, tree strews, lemurs, lorises, bush babies, tarsiers, monkeys, marmosets, macaques, baboons, mandrills, apes, gibbons, orangutans, gorillas, chimpanzees

☛ "reptiles—gila monster, beaded lizard

☛ "snakes—all venomous snakes, snakes over one meter in length, more than three snakes under one meter in length, crocodiles, alligators, caimans, gavials

☛ "birds—ostriches, rheas, cassowaries, emus, kiwis, poultry, fowl

☛ "raptors—hawks, falcons, eagles, buteos, vultures, kites, condors, ospreys, sparrow hawks, owls, all spiders, all venomous insects

☛ "other—all venomous and poisonous animals."

How's that for all-inclusive? And if you did want one of the pets in section five of the same bylaw—which included rabbits, iguanas, gerbils, guinea pigs, hamsters, domesticated mice, domesticated birds (parrots, budgies), ferrets—you had to ensure it was penned at all times and never allowed off your property, and you could not have more than five of these animals "in total, regardless of the species."

I'm *really* curious about which exotic pet during Taber's history might have precipitated the formation of this bylaw!

Man's Best Friend

There was a time when a dog was considered a must-have for most households. It served as a loyal watchdog, kind-hearted companion and all-round good egg. But over time, as the wide variety of dog breeds made their way into the general population, it became clear that select species were a little less desirable than others, at least with some people. Pit bulls, Rottweilers and Doberman pinschers were just a few of the breeds that several communities have banned or have enacted specific bylaws to deal with them.

The city of Grande Prairie, for example, revised its "Vicious and/or Restricted Dog" bylaw in 2007. That community lists pit bull terriers, American pit bull terriers or pit bulls and Staffordshire terriers as "restricted dogs." At one point, residents who owned one of these restricted breeds had to have a minimum of $1,000,000 in liability coverage to cover any potential attacks or injuries caused by the animal.

As a result of the 2007 revision, the vicious and/or restricted status could be lifted if the animal passed the Canadian Kennel Club canine good neighbour evaluation. It appears that dogs that have retained their vicious and/or restricted status must still follow the original guidelines, which include proper penning and strict harness and muzzling when the dogs are in public.

Working Dogs

They might be a necessity for some individuals, and most are already licensed through the organizations they'd previously been affiliated with, but if you live in Banff and own a seeing eye, hearing ear or any other working dog, you still need an animal licence, according to the town's Animal Control Bylaw.

That said, the licence wouldn't cost you a penny, as long as you can prove your pup is necessary and trained. Council passed their latest Animal Control Bylaw in 2008.

Feline Friends

Not everyone is a dog person. Some of us prefer cats. And according to statistics, there are more domestic cats in Canada than there are dogs, partly because cat owners often have more than one kitty in the house. With that in mind, it sounds like Taber's town council might have hit a gold mine in 2003 when they legislated a bylaw that stated cat owners had to license their cats. If the cat was spayed or neutered, the cost was a mere $15.

Of course, as we all know, a lot of cats out there have not been altered by their owners. If that is the case for you, and you live in Taber, you'll be shelling out $85 to license your cat. And if you're bold enough to breed your cat and silly enough to advertise the fact, you need a $100 licence.

At one point, the town had a "trap-neuter-release program" to deal with negligent cat owners who hadn't taken the time to make that all-important vet visit. Furry felines ferreting about looking for a bit of action were captured instead by an animal control officer. They were then taken to the local pound and, if they were in good shape, spayed or neutered. Should the owner want the kitty back, the vet bill had to be paid first. Otherwise, the confiscated cat was offered up for adoption.

Taber is a rare example of a community that has enacted a cat bylaw. One of the reasons for this is that the bylaw is pretty much unenforceable—cats that have owners are not as frequently the problem. It's the stray and feral cats that cause the most nuisances, and it usually costs more money to hunt them down and try to enforce the legislation than any amount of money the administration collects from cat owners who purchase a licence. So all things considered, this is a pretty odd law indeed.

Cat Patrol

Red Deer took a strong stance on its cat population in 1996. City council passed its "Cat Bylaw," outlining the responsibilities of cat owners. This bylaw goes a bit further than the usual ban on cats running loose or damaging another person's property:

☛ Animal control officers have to keep written tabs on the cats they find or the complaints they respond to.

☛ Owners of cats that are repeat offenders are dealt increasingly steep fines.

☛ It is absolutely forbidden for an owner to "interfere with or attempt to obstruct an Animal Control Officer, Peace Officer, or Bylaw Enforcement Officer who is attempting to capture or who has captured any cat in accordance with the provisions of this bylaw."

☛ And furthermore, residents who complain of a stray cat in their neighbourhood can acquire a cat trap from Red Deer's animal control officer and capture the wayward animal themselves.

HUNTING, FISHING AND ALL THINGS WILD

Back in the day, survival often depended on the wild game hubby brought home for supper. If the man of the house wasn't around, any one of the junior men still at home or the woman of the house had to hoist a rifle and take aim.

That way of living might work if you lived in the Westlock or Barrhead district in the early 1900s and claimed squatter's rights on a remote piece of land. But running off haphazardly with your firearm and shooting at any varmint that moved might result in a few ramifications, such as accidently shooting the neighbour's dog—or the neighbour!

This section takes a look at a few of Alberta's old, and some not so old, hunting and fishing laws. For the most part, they make perfect sense. It's just a little shocking that some of these rules had to be legislated in the first place.

Playing Fair with Guns

The Legislative Assembly of the Province of Alberta outlined what it believed were fair and equitable rules and regulations for hunting in their "Game Act," which was passed on March 15, 1907:

☛ You couldn't "hunt, trap, take, shoot at, wound or kill" a bison or buffalo.

☛ Mountain sheep or goats were also off limits before October 1, 1909.

☛ Elk, or wapiti, had a bit of a longer reprieve. You couldn't hunt them until November 1, 1910.

☛ Pronghorn antelope were protected between November 1 and October 1 of the following year, each year—in other words,

hunting season on this animal was restricted to the month of October.

☞ "Any of the deer family, whether known as caribou, moose, deer, or otherwise" could only be hunted during the month of November.

☞ The use of "any poison, opium or other narcotic" to hunt an animal was strictly a no-no.

☞ And you couldn't use "any sunken pants, nightlights, traps, nets or snares of any kind, swivel, spring, automatic or machine shot guns" when hunting.

Since these regulations dealt with big game animals, hunters should have had no difficulty in following the rules. After all, even youngsters know what a moose looks like. However, it was probably a lot trickier to play within the rules when it came to hunting bird species:

☛ Ducks and swans could not be hunted between January 1 and August 23 of each year.

☛ The white-winged Scoter wasn't so lucky. As long as you were hunting in "that portion of the province lying to the north of township 50," these birds were fair game at any time.

☛ Cranes were out of bounds from January 1 to September 1— although I have no idea what could ever entice someone to shoot one of these magnificent creatures.

☛ Rails and coots or any other member of the Rallidae family were also off limits between January 1 and September 1, as were shore birds like the "snipe, sandpiper, plover and curlew."

☛ When it came to "grouse, partridge, pheasant, ptarmigan and prairie chicken," the regulations were about as clear as mud if you ask me:

> *...before the 15th day of September, 1908, and after such date between the first day of November, 1908, and the first day of October, 1909; and between the first day of November and the first day of October in each year thereafter, provided that no English pheasant shall be taken or killed at any time, nor shall more than twenty birds of the family Gallinae be killed by one person in any one day nor more than two hundred in a season; and no person other than a game guardian in respect of game forfeited under the provisions of this Act shall at any time buy, sell, barter or exchange any bird in this subclause mentioned.*

All I can say is, if you weren't buying, selling, bartering or exchanging birds, what on earth were you doing with 200 dead fowl?

Safe Hunting Sanctions

You have to be 12 years old in Alberta to obtain a hunting licence. But there are a lot of other considerations you need to be aware of before you pull the trigger of the new 270 Weatherby Mag you have just unwrapped on Christmas morning. In particular, hunters in Alberta can't use any firearm "that is capable of firing more than one bullet during one pressure of the trigger."

Although donning fluorescent vests and other brightly coloured items isn't a requirement for hunters throughout most of the province, if you plan to hunt on Camp Wainwright, you need to wear such items. However, if you're planning on bow hunting in the same area, you should travel incognito—in other words, sans bright colours.

Good to Know

Most hunters understand that they need to read, digest and actually know the rules surrounding safe and responsible hunting in this province to acquire a hunting licence, but some of the finer points of the legislation might be lost once the written work is complete and an applicant has passed the test. With that in mind, here are a few things you can't do when roaming the wilderness in search of fresh game:

- ☞ Hunt with an arrow "equipped with an explosive head"

- ☞ Use a light when hunting

- ☞ Use live wildlife to lure your prey

- ☞ Use a "poisonous substance or an immobilizing drug"

- ☞ Abandon the meat of any wildlife deemed edible—the carcass of a bear or cougar is exempt from this

- ☞ Shoot a gun "between one-half hour after sunset and one-half hour before sunrise." To gauge this correctly, the Alberta

Guide to Hunting Regulations points you in the direction of the "sunrise/sunset table."

☞ Shoot from a boat, unless it's "propelled by muscular power or is at anchor" or from any aircraft or vehicle "whether it is moving or stationary"—though it's quite difficult to understand why one would shoot from a stationary aircraft.

Hold Your Fire

Population culls might be acceptable in some parts of the province, but it's certainly not something residents of Canmore approve of, regardless how many critters wander its downtown streets. In December 1991, the town passed a bylaw stating it was illegal to hunt or trap wild prey, or "exotic animals," with firearms, bow and arrow, crossbow, slingshot or any other projectile.

Furthermore, to ensure there was no doubt as to what the term "hunting" meant, town council provided an in-depth definition of the term that included a ban on shooting, harassing or worrying the wildlife; chasing, pursuing or stalking; capturing, injuring or killing; or helping anyone else to do any of these things. The fine for breaking this law can cost you $2500 or up to six months in jail if you neglect to pay the piper.

Watching those Wolves

Keeping animal populations in balance is a continuous challenge if the rise and fall of the wolf population in Alberta is any indication. Beginning in 2005, Alberta Sustainable Resource Development has conducted a cull of these animals in an effort to get their numbers down to a manageable size. In the last five years, the authorities have had an aerial view of their prey, courtesy a helicopter ride, making these pelts pretty pricy indeed.

But in 1909, when Alberta's Minister of Agriculture was monitoring this species, hunters were paid a $10 bounty for each timber wolf pelt. Prairie wolf and wolf pup pelts went for a lot less, at a $1 a pop. Once purchased, these pelts became the property of the Alberta government. However, if the pelts you brought in were picked up from anywhere outside of Alberta, you'd lose money—and a lot of it! Fraudulent claims cost the offender a $100 fine. What's not clear, however, is how the authorities would know that the pelt being presented to them was indeed from Alberta?

Work—What Makes the World Go Round

Your work is to discover your world and then with all your heart give yourself to it.

–Hindu Prince Gautama Siddhartha,
the founder of Buddhism, 563–483 BC

NINE TO FIVE AND THEN SOME

To live, we must work. We need money to pay the bills, right? But our work is hopefully more than just about making money. What we do to make a living in some way defines us.

Work also makes the world go around—our global social and economic stability depends on it. Of course, managing such a vast workforce involves intricacies at every turn. And when problems arise, policies or laws are developed to address those problems.

Again, what makes this section particularly interesting is how laws and policies define the world we live in. They offer us a peek into how the issues regarding our workplaces have evolved.

Public Persona

In the early formation of this land we now call Alberta, employment standards didn't merely focus on fair wages and employer responsibilities. And our performance on the job wasn't the only way in which we were judged. In an "Ordinance Respecting Masters and Servants," passed on March 22, 1877, individuals employed as "clerk, journeyman, apprentice, servant, labourer or

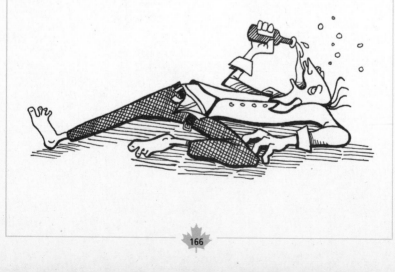

otherwise" who were found "guilty of ill-behaviour, drunkenness, refractory conduct or idleness, of absenting himself by day or night, without leave, from his proper service or employment, or from the house or residence of his employer, of refusing or neglecting to perform his just duties, or to obey the lawful commands of his master, of dissipating his employer's property or effects, or of any unlawful act that may affect his employer's interest" was in big, and I mean *big* trouble. The alleged offender could be hauled up in front of a "Judge, Stipendiary Magistrate or Justice of the Peace" and fined as much as $40 and the costs of prosecution. If you didn't pay—you guessed it! Off to jail you went. And if the courts were really displeased with your behaviour on the job, and you didn't cough up the cash to cover your costs, you could find yourself behind bars for as long as two months.

Furthermore, if you were just trying to be a good friend and were caught harbouring any of the above employees that were AWOL from the workplace, you could be facing the same penalties.

On a Cop's Salary?

It seems the old jest tossed about on evening sitcoms such as *Barney Miller* weren't so far from the truth, even in small town Canada. Innisfail might have been ahead of its neighbours when it came to actually hiring a police constable, but the wage paid to these men in blue was modest at best. In the early 1900s, Innisfail's sole constable earned "$30 per year, plus 10 percent of revenue collected from fines issued." Yikes!

Protecting Children

Although there wasn't a lot of help out there for families struggling to put bread on the table in the early 1900s, Alberta's provincial government was concerned about placing children into the workforce. This was especially true for young boys taking jobs in the growing coalmine industry. Coal was first discovered in this province in 1792, and it wasn't long before the powers that be recognized the kind of coin that could be made in this industry. Folks struggling to make ends meet also knew coal mining was a way to bring in the money they needed, and many families sent their sons to work in the mines.

But in 1906, the province of Alberta acknowledged there were problems with this idea and passed a bylaw requiring these young lads looking to land their first job to be at least 12 years old, literate and "familiar with the rules of arithmetic." That same bylaw disallowed females of any age to work in the coal mining industry.

Minimum Requirements

It made sense that opening up jobs in the coalmines for kids might require a closer look, but in 1909, Edmonton established extensive labour laws for youngsters trying their hand at any job in that city. For example, while it used to be quite common to see very young children selling newspapers, the new bylaws required boys in this position to be at least 10 years of age. Girls, on the other hand, had to be 16 to hold down this prestigious position. The job of "boot-black," otherwise known as a "shoe shiner," carried the same age restrictions.

Once these youngsters reached the approved-upon age, they had to approach city officials with written permission from their school principals providing the youths' school attendance reports, as well as a statement that said the child was "of the normal development of a child of his [or her] age and physically fit for such employment, and that such principal or chief executive officer approves the granting of permit and badge to such child."

After this criterion was met, the city could then give these youths a licence, which came with a badge that made it easy for officials to recognize they were working legally.

Even after all these hoops had been hopped through, young workers had one more restriction—they couldn't work after

9:00 AM or before 6:00 PM. Youth desperate enough to try to break these rules faced a hefty penalty should they get caught. If they were arrested, they were ordered to stand trial in juvenile court.

BETTER BUSINESS AND OTHER LEGALITIES

The cost of doing business is expensive no matter what era of our history you choose to revisit. Once established, every community developed its own set of regulations surrounding the who, what, where, when, why and how of business ownership, and those regulations usually ended up costing business owners a lot of money. Municipal, federal, retail and all other forms of taxation skim any possible profit that new entrepreneurs might dream to recoup from their initial investment. And don't forget the community licence fee. After all, the government providing everything from basic infrastructure to water and sewer and police services need to have a piece of the pie if they want to continue to accommodate these businesses.

For the most part, these regulations are quite logical and are meant to protect the public and share the wealth. Then again, what good could it possibly do to charge youngsters a licence fee to set up a lemonade stand on a street corner? The bylaws in this section give us a glimpse of how communities in Alberta have evolved over the years as well as some of the growing pains experienced along the way.

The Cost of Doing Business

The town of Clifton legislated the sale of foodstuffs such as "fruit-cake, lemon pops and ginger beer" in a bylaw dating back to 1859. The legislation required any enterprising business owners looking to set up their own vendor in the community, and that vendor could be something as simple as setting up a lemonade stand, to purchase a permit from the town. The licence only cost a dollar, and if you consider that the fine for not obtaining the required permission was a hefty $20, it only made sense to get the permit.

The Life of a Butcher

An Ordinance Respecting Hides, passed on November 22, 1889, by the Legislative Assembly of the Territories, detailed the responsibilities of butchers or anyone else who slaughtered cattle:

☛ All butchers were expected to keep detailed records of each animal, its lineage and owner information.

☛ Anyone buying a hide also had to keep a record of the animals.

☛ Slaughtered hides had to be kept at the "place of slaughtering for a period of not less than seven days, and such hides shall be open to the inspection of the public."

☛ Individuals who weren't butchers but had slaughtered a cow were expected by law to also hang the hide for the minimum time period.

☛ No one "other than the owner or his agent or employee [could] skin or remove from the carcass the skin or hide of any neat cattle found dead."

☛ It was against the law to keep the hide of a slaughtered animal "intact for the period of thirty days, subject to the inspection of the public."

Start at the Very Beginning

The first retrievable bylaw in the town of Lethbridge, dated 1891, is aptly called Bylaw 1, and it deals directly with businesses in that community. Hawkers, peddlers and transient traders had to make sure stopping by Lethbridge was worth their while since a licence for them to do business in that town was $100 per year.

For the most part, the amount wasn't out of the realm of licence fees for other businesses except, perhaps, when you consider the income possibility between these businesses. For example, "Liquid Refreshment Houses" paid the same annual fee of $100. But considering they weren't likely transient businesses, and their product and service is what some might consider desirable, it's quite possible their $100 licence fee was well spent.

Transient Traders and Taxation

By 1893, Fort Macleod's council noticed "transient traders" were making their way through the community periodically, and those individuals weren't necessarily paying equitable taxes for the privilege of doing business as they passed through. So the town fathers enacted the following intricate bylaw:

> *No Transient trader or other person occupying premises in the Town of Macleod for temporary periods and whose names have not been entered on the last revised assessment roll of the said Municipality in the respect of income or personal*

*property shall sell goods, wares or merchandise
or offer the same for sale either by auction
conducted by himself or any other person or in
any other manner whatsoever or carry on any
business, trade, profession, occupation or calling
for temporary periods without first having
obtained a license to do so...*

The licence fee for anyone wanting the privilege of doing some
form of "temporary business" in town was $5 per day.

Setting Out Guidelines

In 1901, Cardston made doing business in that community one
of the council's first concerns. If you thought a $100 licence fee
per year was steep for the folks down in Lethbridge, Cardston's
fee was set at $10 a week. If you were a hawker or peddler mov-
ing in and out of that town on a regular basis, it's not inconceiv-
able that you could be paying a year's worth of licences for
10 weeks of business. There was a loophole, however. Businesses
could opt to pay $15 per month, or $25 per quarter.

Farmers, dairy workers and market gardeners selling their produce
within town limits were exempt from having to purchase a business licence. Butchers and meat markets, however, were not given
the same exemption. They paid $25 per year for their licences.

Circuses and "menageries" were slammed with a steep licence fee.
For the privilege of performing in that community, these "businesses" were required to pay "fifty dollars for the first performance and twenty five dollars for each additional performance."

On the other hand, "liquid refreshment houses" only had to pay
the town $25 per year for their licence. Restaurants where these
same beverages were sold paid a $100 fee, and licensed hotels
were charged $200 to do business in any given year, as were
"wholesale liquor houses."

Cutting it Close

In 1901, council members in the south-central community of Cardston decided their business bylaw would include an annual licence fee of $5 per chair for barbers in town. That made for a lot of "shave and a haircut" at two bits a pop before the poor barber even started to make any money.

It Pays to Belong

Insurance wasn't a foreign topic in 1902. Agents peddled their coverage the same way any hawker or peddler did. But the amount of money insurance agents paid the town for the privilege of working there differed depending on whether or not an agent lived in Cardston. Agents who were residents of the town paid $12 per year to conduct their business dealings. Non-resident agents were charged a $25 licence fee.

Paying the Piper

Any businessmen thinking they could cut corners and avoid paying their fair dues to the town of Cardston had another thought coming. In 1901, the town enacted their business bylaw. Not only did the bylaw include details surrounding licence fees and the manner with which they should be paid, but it also provided for the hiring of a town inspector. It was the inspector's job to "make diligent inquiry and examination as to all persons in the town liable to pay licence as required...and shall make a list of the same showing under which heading they are to be classed and the amount payable by each and submit such list to the committee on fire, licence and police from time to time." On September 19, 1901, at the passing of this bylaw, Martin Woolf was appointed as Cardston's first Inspector of Licences.

Overstepping Authority

In a strange turn of events that appeared to have resulted from an ordinance of the North-West Territories, the area government of the time, Cardston's town council repealed their licence bylaw on September 21, 1901, two days after the bylaw had first come into effect. The detailed bylaw was replaced with a shorter, more concise bylaw. It appears that the town wasn't able to charge licence fees on a weekly, monthly and quarterly basis if that amount exceeded the total annual charge so the town decided to amend its bylaw.

A Growing Concern

In 1906, Hardisty had just received hamlet status, and five years later, that was followed by a new town designation. By then, the community boasted a growing population, and along with an increase in residents, amenities such as a school, an arcade, a hall and a place for area farmers to unwind with a tall, cold beverage after a long day in the fields were something quite desirable.

Of course, all of this required some form of monitoring, especially when it came to businesses selling liquor. And so in 1911, the town council passed a bylaw enabling them to hire a licence inspector whose primary responsibility it was to "visit and inspect every licensed place for the sale of liquor within the Town, and to prosecute forthwith for every case of infraction of the provisions of the Liquor License Ordinance..." A fellow by the name of Alexander Mursell landed the job at the generous salary of $5 per month. There is no mention of fringe benefits.

Oh, and in case you were wondering, a liquor licence in Hardisty at that time in the town's history cost $200.

Taboo on Tobacco

Magrath was onto something fairly early on in Alberta's history. On April 5, 1911, the council of that municipality passed a bylaw restricting the sale of tobacco to minors under the age of 16 years.

Breaking the law could cost the offender a fine of up to $10 or 10 days in jail, with or without hard labour.

Minors could purchase tobacco products for their mom or dad with a signed letter indicating that the purchase was for the parent. And although picture ID wasn't around back then, if a shopkeeper didn't believe a patron was 16 years or older, he or she could require the individual to provide "evidence that he is in fact over that age."

Protecting the Public

Hardisty clearly thought of more than just making money when it came to establishing new businesses in its community. The town was also concerned about protecting its citizens from businesses that might pose a health or safety risk in certain areas. And on November 13, 1911, the council enacted Bylaw 28, restricting any "livery, Board and sales stable, Hand laundry, Second hand or Junk store, Blacksmiths shop and for shoeing forge" from doing business in certain locations: "…that part of Block 2 facing Churchill street the whole of Block 3, those parts of Blocks 6 & 7 facing Churchill street and that part of Railway Avenue comprising Blocks 1, 2, & 3."

I can understand the possible health and safety concerns associated with a business like a blacksmith shop or livery stable, but it's difficult to see how a "Second hand or Junk store" would fall into that category. Someone must have brought this to the council's attention because an amendment to the bylaw deleted that reference. At its inception, the bylaw did not provide for a grandfather clause for businesses of this type that might have already been operating in those areas.

Overture, Curtain, Lights…

In November 1911, Hardisty officially licensed the Orange Hall Company to be used for theatrical purposes. By paying the grand total of $37.50 per year, the proprietors of the building were "permitted to use the said Hall for Theatrical and other Entertainments without contravening any of the conditions of By-Law No. 3, section 4, subsection 4…" The clause from that earlier bylaw legislated a $5-per-day licence fee for "Theatrical or Musical performances."

That original bylaw also restricted any "circus or menagerie or both combined" to pitch a tent and entertain residents before first putting out the necessary $25 required for the licence fee. Hawkers and peddlers were also addressed under this bylaw. Along with the necessary licence, hawkers and peddlers couldn't sell "Agricultural products, nor to the selling of goods at whole-sale to merchants of this Town, nor to the selling of coal, fuel and fish."

Merchants operating pool and billiard halls or owners of a bowl-ing alley were charged an annual fee of $10 for the first table or lane and $5 for the second and/or subsequent table or lane.

The Pains of Being a Pro

Slap together a talent night at the local hall and it's all fun and games, but if you were a seasoned actor and showed up in Ponoka in 1914, you had to pay for the privilege of strutting your stuff. According to a bylaw passed that year, any "actor, performer, troupe, or company of actors, or other theatrical or dramatical performance where an admission fee is charged" had to pay a $10 licence fee for each performance day. A "travelling circus, menagerie, hippodrome, dog or pony show, or any other like travelling exhibits" faced an even stiffer fee of $50 a day, but this didn't seem to cover all the costs involved in these perfor-mances. If these shows wanted a licence to "exhibit circus riding, rope walking, rope dancing, tumbling or other acrobatic or gymnastics or acrobatic performances" or "novelties, wonderful animals or other side shows usually exhibited by show men," they had to pay an additional $10 per exhibit.

Licence Fees

The cost of doing business in the central town of Coronation in 1912 was $100 per year, which seems quite steep for those days when compared with the amounts other communities charged. This licence fee applied to all trade and businesspersons operating within town limits, with variations applied as council saw fit.

A Fishy Situation

There must have been a high demand for fish in Ponoka in 1914. That year, the council passed an extensive bylaw that dealt with many issues, one of which was charging a licence fee for any

"pedler [sic] or dealer of fish who does not maintain a place of business within the Town of Ponoka."

While most business licences were issued on an annual basis, transient fish peddlers had to pay a $12.50 licence for each of the following six-month periods: from January 1 to June 30, and from July 1 to December 31. All other "transient businesses in premises occupied or rented for less than one month, where goods or merchandise are offered for sale by private sale, auction sale, or in any other manner" were charged an annual fee of $50.

A Weighty Issue

Keeping up to consumer demand was only one of the concerns Edmonton bakers dealt with on a daily basis in 1913. An old city bylaw instituted strict measures when it came to the criteria local dough punchers had to follow when baking bread. For example, there were two main weight restrictions for loaves of bread: one pound (680 grams) or three pounds (1.36 kilograms). Fancy breads were the exception to this rule. They were supposed to weigh 21 ounces (595 grams).

City inspectors routinely toured Edmonton's bakeries, checking bread weight. Depending on whether the chap was in a good mood on any given day, he might make a slight allowance for weight variance, especially if the bread had been out of the oven for some time. On the other hand, delivering the baked goods was more strictly regulated. The baker had to provide and use "baskets for the handling of bread, and shall instruct all employees to do the same."

Keeping Tabs on Booze

According to the Liquor Export Act of 1918, no one in Alberta could "have, expose, or keep liquor for export or sale" unless that liquor was being kept "in a bonded liquor warehouse." These facilities could not be in any location outside of "an incorporated city." The Liquor Export Act was one of Alberta's earliest attempts at regulating liquor after the province enacted Prohibition on July 1, 1916. Following a plebiscite on the issue, Prohibition ended in 1923.

Hand Over the Cash

The village of Coaldale enacted a bylaw in 1920 dealing with business licences within their community. Anyone advertising a fee for a service or running a business in Coaldale had to pay for the privilege, but unlike other communities, the fee was not the same for everyone.

An auctioneer coughed up $25 for the right to work in Coaldale. Billiard rooms had to pay $10 per year if they had one pool table, an additional $5 for the second table and $2.50 for each subsequent table. Draymen paid $25 to run a two-horse team and an extra $5 for each subsequent team. Hawkers and peddlers were charged $10 for a licence, as were insurance agents. Ice cream parlours paid $5 to run their business year-round, but if someone wanted to set up an ice cream stand for a single day, it cost the vendor one dollar. Laundries paid an annual fee of $5, restaurants or "lunch counters," livery and feed stables put out $10 to do business each year. But the biggest fee any businessperson had to pay in order to do business in Coaldale was $50. Real estate agents were the lucky lot to draw that straw. This bylaw was on the books until it was finally repealed in September 2001.

Keeping the Clutter Down

The obstruction of sidewalks and alleyways became enough of a growing concern in Beiseker that its local council saw fit to enact a bylaw prohibiting sidewalk obstruction. The to-the-point bylaw was anything but loquacious, but it left no room for doubt: "…no one shall store goods of any kind on any side-walks or alley-ways for a longer period of time than that [sic] necessary to remove same to place of business and in no instance to exceed one hour." The law was passed on April 30, 1921.

One-armed Wonder

I'll bet you didn't know that slot machines have been around since 1887? That's when San Francisco native Charles Fey created the devilish machines. It wasn't long before this poor man's promise gained notoriety and appeared across North America. And by 1924, Alberta instituted an act regarding the use of slot machines in the province.

Simply put—they were illegal. No one—business owner or otherwise—was allowed to "keep or operate, or permit to be kept or operated upon any premises or in any place, any slot machine," period. If a police officer discovered a slot machine, the owner or essee was served with notice that it had to be removed within seven days. If that didn't happen, the officer could seize the offending machine.

Strangely enough, the act states that the owner of the slot machine could appeal the action if evidence was provided that proved the property in question was not, in actual fact, a slot machine. The owner could also produce evidence showing that the slot machine "should not be confiscated." However, there is no explanation outlining possible arguments that would change the verdict.

Holy Orders

The United Church of Canada was inaugurated on June 10, 1925, at which time the Methodist Church, Congregational Union of Canada and 70 percent of the Presbyterian Church presence in this country joined to form the new denomination. But more than a year earlier, on April 12, 1924, Alberta passed "An Act respecting the Union of certain Churches" addressing the change. While the participating parties ironed out the spiritual issues, the act focused primarily on the amalgamation of property that was once owned by each denomination individually and the co-ownership of that property.

Not for Display

On August 10, 1931, Edmonton city council passed a business bylaw that addressed what some residents might have considered distasteful. By that time in the province's history, Edmonton had enjoyed the prestige of serving as the provincial capital city for almost three decades, it had established the country's first licensed airfield and it was being hailed by some as the gateway to the north. The Wild West image of Alberta, and most of North America for that matter, was fast fading into memory. And as a burgeoning, civilized community, it was deemed unnecessary for people to buy the guns and knives they might have once carried on a regular basis.

With this in mind, council's new bylaw forbid shop owners to "display any pistol, revolver, dirk, dagger, bowie knife, stiletto, metal knuckles, skull cracker, slug shot or other offensive weapon of a like character" in their show windows. If you were in the market to purchase one or more of these items, you had to ask the retailer to show them to you in private. The law was on the books until 1996, when it was finally repealed.

Wanna Buy a Watch?

Laws dealing with "hawkers and peddlers" have been around for centuries in this country. According to one source, as many as 666 individuals were working full time as hawkers and peddlers in Canada in 1871. But it wasn't until 1933 that Beiseker enacted legislation to govern, regulate and license these unique business people.

Bylaw 12A came into effect on April 27 of that year and required these individuals to pay a $5 licence fee to do business in Beiseker. The licence was only provided to hawkers and peddlers who already held a provincial licence, and it expired on December 31 of each year.

Got Gas?

Let's face it, all levels of government run on the taxes they accu-mulate, and a good part of the business they conduct surrounds the collection of those taxes. The bigger the industry, the more tax money the government hopes to collect. On April 7, 1936, Alberta passed an "Act to Provide for Imposing a Tax on Fuel Oil," leaving no doubt to business folks and consumers alike what was expected:

☛ Any "substance or liquid whatsoever" used to power an engine would be defined as "fuel."

☛ The rate of tax was assessed at "seven cents a gallon on all fuel oil."

- Anyone who bought or used fuel oil without the assessed taxes being paid by the seller was responsible for paying the "Minister for the use of His Majesty in the right of the Province of Alberta a charge or tax" at that same rate.

- The only exemption to the tax was the fuel used to drive a vehicle, power a boat or fly across provincial boundaries.

- And if an individual was believed to possess fuel oil "upon which the tax payable in pursuance of this Act has not been paid..." they would be "liable on summary conviction to a penalty of not less than one hundred dollars and costs, and not more than five hundred dollars and costs."

The act does not explain how an inspector could tell if the fuel oil being used in any given case came from this province or elsewhere, or whether the tax was indeed collected.

Protecting Our Petroleum

It could be argued that there is no larger industry in this province than the oil and gas industry, and the government of Alberta worked to protect this natural resource as early as 1938. That's the year Alberta's political powers passed the "Act for the Conservation of the Oil and Gas Resources of the Province of Alberta."

The purpose of this piece of legislation was to control or regulate "the production of oil or gas or both, whether by restriction or prohibition and whether generally or with respect to any specified area or any specified well or wells or by repressuring of any oil field, gas field or oil gas field and, incidentally thereto, providing for the compulsory purchase of any well or wells." A board overseeing this industry was formed, and its members were given strict instruction that they were not to have any "monetary interest of any description, directly or indirectly, in any property or in any business or undertaking carried on for the purpose of searching for, winning or getting, or for the purpose of gathering, collecting, processing, handling or distributing any petroleum in the Province." No chance for conflict of interest in this legislation.

Milk Money

In November 1939, Coaldale passed a bylaw regulating the sale of milk and cream to its residents. The new legislation required anyone in the dairy business in and around Coaldale to provide a "certificate of sanitary inspection from the Provincial government" to the local village office and to also purchase a $5 licence. The fine for conducting your dairy business without a licence was $10, plus the "costs of action." There's no doubt regulations surrounding the dairy industry grew and changed repeatedly throughout the years, and this law wasn't repealed until September 2001.

Closed?

Although it wasn't uncommon for businesses in small communities to close their doors for all or part of one day of the week, a bylaw passed in the community of Berwyn in 1942 leaves today's readers a bit confused. For some unexplained reason, the village council passed a bylaw legislating that all businesses must remain closed every Wednesday from noon until 2:00 AM the following morning. These business closures were effective between May 20 and August 12.

Setting Up Shop

Picture Butte moved from hamlet to village status in 1943. Once a village government was established, the new leaders set about outlining the dos and don'ts for their community. Among the first issues up to the plate were the regulations related to business operations, namely the hours businesses in town were allowed to operate. It's no surprise that Picture Butte joined other communities in the province in declaring that their shops had to be closed during public holidays. However, the wording of this section of the bylaw might have required legal advice to follow correctly:

> *Except where otherwise specified in or provided for by the By-law all 'shops' shall be closed at six o'clock in the afternoon of each weekday, excepting Saturday and shall remain closed from six o'clock in the afternoon of each weekday excepting Saturday until five o'clock in the forenoon of the next following day. Provided that on Saturday of each week all shops may remain open until nine o'clock in the afternoon, but shall be closed at nine o'clock in the afternoon, and remain closed during the following Sunday and until five o'clock in the forenoon of the following Monday and provided further that when Saturday of any week is a public holiday, all shops may remain open until nine o'clock in the afternoon of Friday of such week; and provided further that on the two week days immediately preceding Christmas day all shops may remain open until nine o'clock in the afternoon of each such day.*

Huh?

Mmm, Mmm, Good

We've all heard that adequate milk consumption is important to our diet. And nothing beats a glass of milk and cookies—just ask Santa! For people who were raised on a dairy farm or bought milk from a dairy farmer in the good old days before pasteurization was mandatory, a glass of farm-fresh milk was even better than the packaged version we buy in today's supermarkets. Sadly, many of us never experience the difference. Over the years, legislation enacted across the province and throughout Canada outlawed the sale of unpasteurized milk. Some communities bucked the trend a little longer than others. It wasn't until 1989 that Grande Prairie's city council passed a bylaw forbidding the sale of unpasteurized milk.

Mixing Booze with the Law

Once communities instituted the requirements for all businesses to purchase a business licence in order to operate lawfully, distinctions were made between business types. A hawker and peddler paid different licence fees than drinking establishments did—even back in the earliest days of the settlement of this province, booze brought in the money, and town fathers knew it. But as communities and the businesses they contained grew, councils and administrations in Alberta instituted other rules and regulations. It was no longer good enough to just purchase a business licence.

It's with that kind of forethought that Red Deer's city council enacted its newest bylaw in 2004 to "Regulate and License Drinking Establishments." Spelled out in the bylaw is the recognition that this community acknowledged "a significant increase in problems associated with the use of Drinking Establishments by patrons." Some of the more innovative regulations that the city included in their bylaw to deal with some of these problems, such as disorderly conduct and vandalism, were:

☞ Details must be provided about any events that might be hosted at a particular drinking establishment.

☞ Any changes to the ownership or purpose of such a business must be reported within 30 days.

☞ First aid must be available for patrons on site, as well as security personnel and surveillance cameras.

☞ The building itself must be constructed in such a way that noise doesn't filter into city streets.

☞ The owner and manager also had to "install, maintain and operate an airport-style metal detecting security gate of a model and type and in a manner specified by the Inspections and Licensing Manager, for the purpose of identifying and barring entry to anyone carrying metal weapons."

☞ In addition, these establishments had to follow up with any additional requirements that the inspections and licensing manager might determine necessary after any inspection.

Taking a Hard Stand

A growing concern over the instances of drinking and driving in and around Wetaskiwin propelled city aldermen to enact strict guidelines for what they defined as "liquor retail establishments." In 2009, council tried to push through Bylaw 1753-09, restricting the sale of liquor to between 10:00 AM and 8:00 PM on weekdays, weekends and statutory holidays, inclusive. In addition, off-sales establishments were confined to doing business during that same time period. And anyone providing a liquor delivery service had to ensure the booze was in the customer's hands by 8:30 PM. Penalties for breaching these guidelines were stiff: the offender could expect a fine ranging from $1000 to $10,000.

Of course, such strict rules and enforcement was bound to raise hackles in the community, especially when you consider that a 10-minute drive down the highway took you to a small community where four liquor stores were willing to serve you until much later than 8:00 PM. In the end, council amended their plans and compromised a little. And on January 1, 2010, the bylaw came into effect, with the closing time for liquor stores changed to 10:00 PM and liquor delivery services to 10:30 PM. Fines for non-compliance were reduced slightly. Business owners were fined $1000 should they sell booze outside the legislated hours. The fines for a second and third offence are $2500 and $5000, respectively.

Liquor Bylaw Fallout

The changes to the portion of Wetaskiwin's business bylaw that dealt with the sale of liquor had an impact on one other retail and service business in that city. In that same bylaw, pawnbrokers found themselves with open and close time regulations as well. According to Bylaw 1753-09, as of January 1, 2010, pawnshops could only open for business between 9:00 AM and 6:00 PM. (Prior to this legislation, pawnshop owners could regulate their own hours, and on some days of the week, like Friday, the doors were often kept open until 9:00 PM.)

The thinking behind that portion of the bylaw was, in the minds of some council members, directly tied to the purchase of liquor. During one council meeting, Alderman Barry Hawkes explained that in his understanding, through discussing the issue with some pawnbrokers, it was not uncommon for individuals to "pawn their kid's clothing, they pawn their kid's bike, they pawn anything they can in order to get their fix." While there was considerable opposition to these business hour restrictions, this portion of the proposed bylaw was not altered.

Policing the Taxi Industry

A new bylaw dealing with the taxi industry passed its third and final reading by Peace River's town council on April 26, 2010. The new legislation outlines all the usual fine print about owning and operating a business in that community, but section four of the bylaw deals directly with cabbies and the requirements they must have to hold that position. And that's where this bylaw gets interesting. Before you can work as a cabbie, you, of course, need a "Taxicab Driver's Permit." However, if you had the following black marks against your name, you were out of luck when it came to acquiring said permit and, consequently, ever working as a cabbie in Peace River:

☛ Convicted of a sexual offence, homicide, kidnapping or abduction, robbery or extortion within five years of applying for the Taxicab Driver's Permit

☛ Convicted of a drug offence with a penalty of three years in jail or longer within the five years prior to applying for said permit

☛ Currently facing charges under the Controlled Drugs and
  Substances Act or convicted of "a number of offences under
  the Traffic Safety Act (and associated regulations) resulting
  in the assessment of ten (10) or more demerit points"

Somehow, just knowing that Peace River had to institute a law
like this makes me a little leery to trust any cabbie before I first
check to see if my community has a similar bylaw.

Filling the Gap

It appears Bentley must have had bylaws in place that, should
they be disregarded by a member of the community, didn't actually cost the offending party any fine or jail time. In other words,
you could blatantly ignore these bylaws and suffer no conse-
quence. So in July 1944, the village fathers passed Bylaw
No. 83/44 to rectify the situation. This bylaw effectively
addressed all previous bylaws that did not contain a penalty
by adding the following clause:

Any person found guilty of an infraction of this By-law shall be liable upon summary conviction, to a fine of not less than One Dollar ($1.00) and not more than Twenty-five Dollars ($25.00), together with the costs of the conviction. Any person failing to pay the amount of such fine and costs shall be liable to imprisonment in the Provincial Jail for a period not exceeding thirty (30) days.

Talk about backtracking!

HOLIDAYS AND THE SABBATH

There was a time when Sundays were sacred. Families worked hard all week and looked forward to a day of rest—a day when the world around them shut down and everyone paused, if only for a few short hours. There's a lot to be said for slowing down and taking time to smell the roses. And if we're to really live, it's important we learn how to chill out, breathe deeply, hold onto some calm.

At the same time, closing the doors of every business on a prescribed day of the week is no longer logical. There needs to be a flow to society's work and rest schedule, and through the years, municipalities have struggled with how to best accommodate that need for balance in life.

What follows are a few examples of just how difficult that's been over the years, and how communities today still wrestle with the question of legislating work hours and regulating exactly what the public at large is allowed to do during any given holiday or day of the week. Sometimes laughable, often illogical, but always instituted with the most serious of intentions, the following bylaws give us a glimpse into the struggles of our ancestors— struggles that continue to this day.

Off Limits

In 1902, Cardston's town council passed a bylaw outlawing the use of billiards, pool and bagatelle tables every day from midnight to 7:00 AM and all day on Sunday. The bylaw doesn't explain the motives for the legislation.

Keep It Holy

For the residents of Hardisty, it was a simple fact that Sunday was the Sabbath Day and must be kept holy. In case anyone wasn't clear on this, the town fathers enacted legislation in 1911 spelling out all the details: no one, or almost no one, was allowed to work on Sunday. Period. The only exception to this were individuals conducting "works of necessity or charity." Nothing more needed to be said.

The Definition of Profanity

If you thought for a moment that small towns and villages had the corner on banning activities on Sundays, and the governments of larger cities, or even the province, might be more liberal in their approach, think again. In 1922, the province of Alberta reinforced earlier laws created in 1898 in their "Act to Prevent the Profanation of the Lord's Day."

Simply put, the law states that no "merchant, tradesman, artificer, mechanic, workman, labourer or other person whatsoever shall on the Lord's Day sell or publicly show forth or expose or offer for sale or purchase any goods, chattels or other personal property or any real estate whatsoever, or do or exercise any worldly labour, business or trade of his ordinary calling; travelling or conveying travellers or His Majesty's mails, selling drugs and medicines and other works of necessity and works of charity only excepted."

Along with being forbidden to work, you couldn't have any fun either. No playing games of any kind. No pool playing or billiards. No races—not on foot, horseback or by vehicle. And betting on these activities was absolutely banned. No firing a gun—unless you were dying of starvation and a grouse waddled by.

Furthermore, "all sales and purchases and all contracts and agreements for sale or purchase of any real or personal property

whatsoever made by any person or persons on the Lord's Day shall be utterly null and void." Ouch!

The penalty for breaking any part of this law was $100 plus the cost of prosecution.

Making Merry

Back in 1945, the folks down in Magrath knew how a little leisure time could lift spirits and build community. On July 16 of that year, the town council passed three readings of Bylaw 444, which proclaimed that Tuesday, the 24th of that month, was to be declared a civic holiday. The bylaw does not indicate the reason for the holiday, and it appears to have been a one-time deal.

No Work, No Play

My mother tells a story about how one preacher in the small town where she grew up frowned on people playing sports on Sunday. He was so adamant about what he considered the ultimate sacrilege that he'd often make an example of one of his flock who had the audacity to commit such a transgression.

As the church organist, my mother would play "Just as I am Without One Plea" as one repeat offender was instructed to creep up the centre aisle of the church on his knees and repeatedly promise not to play hockey on Sunday. Of course, following the service, that same boy returned to the ice rink and laced up his skates for yet another round of shots, passes and body checks.

Although it wasn't against the law to play hockey on Sunday in my mother's hometown, it wasn't something people in general approved of. Other communities, like Cochrane, for example, took their disapproval a step further. In 1950, that town's council passed a bylaw restricting sport activities until after 1:30 PM.

They expanded on exactly which activities could be played on Sunday. This list included the all-time favourites of baseball, softball, fastball, football, rugby, soccer, hockey, lacrosse, tennis, badminton, swimming, track and field, bowling, curling and figure skating. If your sport of choice didn't fit into this list of activities, you'd have to settle for a match on any other day of the week because Sunday was off limits to you!

In Memoriam

The City of Edmonton passed a bylaw on February 11, 1952, declaring February 15, 1952, a civic holiday of sorts. Aside from essential services, all businesses and industries in the city were to remain closed in an effort to encourage residents to spend the day in mourning for King George VI, who passed away on February 6 of that year. He was buried in St. George's Chapel, Windsor Castle, on February 15. He was only 56 when he died, but he'd already served in the capacity of King of the United Kingdom and the British Dominions for 16 years. Although the bylaw dealt with a one-time occurrence, it wasn't repealed until 1996.

Sundays Are Sacred

Making money on the Sabbath was strictly forbidden in the community of Falher as recently as 1954. Even gas stations at that point in the community's history were expected to remain closed. But as the automobile increasingly replaced horsepower, it was soon deemed a necessity to make fuel available to drivers who might find themselves stranded with no gas and without any other means of travel. So that year, Falher's town council passed a bylaw allowing one gas station to open its doors for business each Sunday. Because there was more than one gas station in town, each station took a turn at providing the much-needed service. Those stations that were closed were expected to post a notice on their front door pointing customers to the location of the service station open that day. Should a station owner mistakenly open for business on a Sunday when it wasn't his turn, the village constable fined him $5 for the first offence, $25 for the second and $100 for the third and subsequent offences.

Happy Holiday!

Bowden decided to get in on all the action during Alberta's Golden Jubilee year by declaring a special holiday—which, considering this wasn't done anywhere else in the province as far as the information available supports, makes the holiday at the very least, unique. Wednesday, August 17, 1955, was proclaimed a civic holiday, with all the appropriate community festivities in place, to help "augment the importance of the Alberta Golden Jubilee and the success of the Gigantic Community Picnic."

Off-track Betting Still Off Limits

As recently as 1968, sports that had a tendency to encourage some manner of gambling or that were just outright mean and distasteful to some people were still off limits as far as Sunday recreation went.

For example, that year, Falher passed a bylaw allowing assorted sporting activities, as well as some activities such as air and car shows, to be held on the day of rest. Other pastimes, however, were still on the black list, such as "horse races, or horse race meetings, dog races, boxing contests or exhibitions of wrestling or other like contests or exhibitions."

A Time to Remember

Medicine Hat takes the responsibility of remembering Canada's veterans to heart. So much so that in 1985, the town council passed a bylaw restricting the kind of businesses that could stay open on November 11, and the exact times in which they could serve the public. Between the hours of 9:00 AM and 12 noon, "any shop or business wherein any class of retail business or wholesale business is carried on shall be and remain closed." The public could not enter these retail businesses during those hours, and goods and services offered for sale at the establishments could not be sold. Of course, as with any bylaw, there are always exceptions to the rule. One might wonder, after reading through some of the following exceptions, if there were any businesses left to remain closed:

☞ Drug stores dispensing prescription drugs

☞ Businesses selling food, especially if the "total area used for serving the public or for selling or displaying to the public in the establishment is less than 300 square metres"

☞ Tourist establishments as well as businesses licensed to sell liquor under the Liquor Control Act

☞ And finally, any business selling one or more of the "classes of goods or services set out in Schedule 'A'" of the bylaw could remain open. In case you're wondering, and I know you are, Schedule "A" includes 13 items that cover everything from the sale of handicrafts to flowers, magazines and cigarettes. If you've misread the bylaw and are one of the businesses unfortunate enough to be excluded from the exceptions and stay open for business during the restricted hours, you can expect a fine of up to $1000 for a first offence.

Leading the Way

Alberta was the first province to formally set aside a day to celebrate the family. Aptly known as "Family Day," the first official holiday was declared on the third Monday in February 1990. In keeping with the theme, several communities throughout the province offer free activities to provide families with an affordable way to enjoy their day. It wasn't until 2007 that Saskatchewan joined Alberta in setting aside a day in February for the same purpose. Ontario came on board with the idea in 2008.

What's unique about this holiday, and the law that made it so, was the urban legend surrounding the real reason for the celebration. Some people still talk about the theory that Family Day exists simply because there's such a long stretch between the New Year's Day holiday and Easter. After all, we hard-working folks need a break a whole lot sooner than what in some years can stretch into an almost four-month span between that extra day off!

Special Designations

There are so many things to celebrate in life, and while every day can't be a holiday, governments across this country have traditionally seen fit to create special designations for particular days of the year. One of Alberta's most unique designations has to do with the outdoors.

September 22, 2007, marked the first Provincial Hunting Day in Alberta. Ted Morton, Minister of Sustainable Resource Development at that time, explained the motivation for the special recognition: "We're losing the next generation of hunters to television, computers and shopping malls....We hope that

Provincial Hunting Day will give young Albertans the opportunity to experience the outdoors and build greater respect for wildlife."

Since then, the fourth Saturday of every September has been set aside for this purpose. And we can all join in with Ted Morton and the colleagues of his day in giving thanks that on one Saturday of the year. At least some of our youngsters will gain a "greater respect for wildlife," even though that might mean learning how to shoot a deer instead of rushing out to the mall!

YOU CAN ALWAYS COUNT ON TAXES

Peruse any community's collection of bylaws and you'll quickly discover a large portion of them deal with money. In particular, these bylaws address the cost of providing their citizens with a necessary service—like sewer and water, for example. It doesn't take a rocket scientist to know the money to pay for those services has to come from somewhere. And so communities, municipalities and the province divided their populations, took into account all these services and decided on a tax figure they could, or should, reasonably charge residents.

While it's pretty straightforward really, throughout the years many communities imposed some pretty interesting, and some-times complicated, rules regarding the details behind some of their tax laws. As well, these laws chronicle a time when clearly it cost a lot less to live, but those few dollars a family needed to pay the piper were equally hard to come by.

Rebate? Did You Say Rebate?

Cardston gave their taxpayers a bit of a break, according to Bylaw 114, which was passed on July 22, 1907. The mill rate that year was "twelve (12) mills on the Dollar of the assessed value of the property for general purposes." Another "five and one half mills on the dollar" was tacked on to all assessable property within town limits "for the payment of the interest on the debentures issued by the town..." Another tax of "five (5) cents per lineal foot" was imposed on property "fronting or abutting on any street lane or public highway which is traversed by the water-works system."

However, folks who managed to meet these requirements and pay their tax bill before November 1 of that year were offered a 10 percent rebate. On the other hand, if you were late and hadn't paid your taxes when they were due, you were "deemed to be in default." The bylaw did not address the penalty for being "in default" of your taxes.

The Cost of Education

If you were a business owner, landowner or income earner of any sort in Daysland in 1908, your days of taking home your gross pay were curtailed forever. That year, the town council enacted their municipal and school tax bylaw, requiring anyone who fit into any of these categories to pay their fair share. If you were a man aged 21 and older and earned any kind of income, you were still required to pay an annual poll tax of $2.

Tax Cops

A $1 labour tax was instituted for all male residents aged 21 to 60 in Cochrane once that town's council passed their tax bylaw in 1914. This labour tax was due annually on May 1 and was collected by the local chief of police. Council afforded their cop-turned-tax-collector "all necessary means" to successfully complete the task.

ABOUT THE ILLUSTRATORS

Roger Garcia

Roger Garcia is a self-taught artist with some formal training who special-izes in cartooning and illustration. He is an immigrant from El Salvador, and during the last few years, his work has been primarily cartoons and editorial illustrations in pen and ink. Recently, he has started painting once more. Focusing on simplifying the human form, he uses a bright minimal palette and as few elements as possible. His work can be seen in newspapers, magazines, promo material and on www.rogergarcia.ca.

Peter Tyler

Peter is a recent graduate of the Vancouver Film School's Visual Art and Design and Classical animation programs. Though his ultimate passion is in filmmaking, he is also intent on developing his draftsmanship and storytelling, with the aim of using those skills in future filmic misadventures.

Patrick Hénaff

Born in France, Patrick Hénaff is mostly self-taught. He is a versatile artist who has explored a variety of media under many different influences. He now uses primarily pen and ink to draw, and then processes the images on computer. He is particularly interested in the narrative power of pictures and tries to use them as a way to tell stories.

Roly Wood

Roly has worked in Toronto as a freelance illustrator, and was also employed in the graphic design department of a landscape architecture firm. In 2004, he wrote and illustrated a historical comic book set in Lang Pioneer Village near Peterborough, Ontario. To see more of Roly's work, visit www.rolywood.com.

Pat Bidwell

Pat has always had a passion for drawing and art. Initially self-taught, Pat completed art studies in visual communication in 1986. Over the years, he has worked both locally and internationally as an illustrator/product designer and graphic designer, collecting many awards for excellence along the way. When not at the drawing board, Pat pursues other interests solo and/or with his wife, Lisa.

ABOUT THE AUTHOR

Lisa Wojna

Lisa Wojna, author and co-author of more than 25 other non-fiction books, has worked in the community newspaper industry as a writer and journalist and has travelled all over Canada, from the windy prairies of Manitoba to northern British Columbia, and even to the wilds of Africa. Although writing and photography have been a central part of her life for as long as she can remember, it's the people behind every story that are her motivation and give her the most fulfillment.